THE
Archive Photographs
SERIES

AROUND
MIDDLESBROUGH

THE
Archive Photographs
SERIES

AROUND
MIDDLESBROUGH

Compiled by
Paul Menzies

CHALFORD

First published 1997
Copyright © Paul Menzies, 1997

The Chalford Publishing Company
St Mary's Mill, Chalford,
Stroud, Gloucestershire, GL6 8NX

ISBN 0 7524 0729 5

Typesetting and origination by
The Chalford Publishing Company
Printed in Great Britain by
Bailey Print, Dursley, Gloucestershire

I would like to dedicate this book to:
Ron Newitt
James (Jimmy) Carter
Lauren Kirtley
and John Lindbergh

Acknowledgements

I would like to offer thanks in particular to Bill Bandeira, Cleveland County
Archives Department, Cleveland County Council Department of Planning,
Marianne Deans, the late Jean Duckett, the Evening Gazette Teesside, the late
John Lindbergh, Wilf Mannion, Trevor Miles and Countryside Publications,
Middlesbrough Reference Library - in particular Larry Bruce, Ordnance
Survey, Jeffrey Wilkinson and his family who gave unstintingly of their time
and any other persons who have either knowingly or otherwise given their
help to this work. I would also like to commend the continuing work of
members of the Cleveland and Teesside Local History Society who strive to
continue interest in the history of Middlesbrough - articles in their bulletins
proved invaluable in the research for this work.

Contents

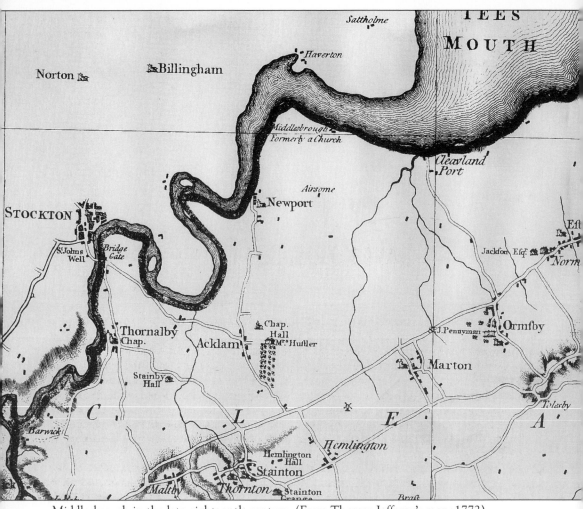

Middlesbrough in the late eighteenth century. (From Thomas Jefferey's map, 1772)

Introduction

Normally local history publications begin with an introduction which includes a chronological history of the subject matter of the book. However, as many readers reading this work will be largely aware of the history of Middlesbrough, this custom is being dispensed with as it is felt unnecessary to reiterate material in this way. The chronological history of the town has not been totally ignored, but as this work tends to adopt a thematic rather than a chronological approach, aspects relating to the history of Middlesbrough are included as part of the text where considered appropriate to the visual sources. Consequently this introduction will discuss the rationale behind writing the book, giving a brief insight into how it came to be put together.

Writing a book on Middlesbrough is a very difficult task, a reflection on the number of excellent publications already written rather than the complexity of research. Publications to date deal with a broad variety of features of the history of the town and it is appropriate to pay tribute to those authors, including Norman Moorsom, Robin Cook, Bob Woodhouse and Arif Chokran, all of whom have produced some excellent material on Middlesbrough. Their work has simultaneously proved to be both an inspiration and rigorous taskmaster impelling me to constantly review this book to ensure that the reader is being offered something new. Yet this need is juxtaposed with the demand to include material readers would expect to find in any book pertaining to deal with the history of Middlesbrough, such as the Transporter Bridge and the Town Hall. Images of these have appeared in many books but to not include them would render the book less than complete.

So why write another book on Middlesbrough? Firstly I have a very personal interest in Middlesbrough. My mother, grandparents and a whole part of my family have been a part of the town throughout this century; my wife and my mother in law come from the town too. Secondly the rapid changes during recent years, resulting in the disappearance of much of the old town, have greatly enhanced the general interest in the town's past. Even in my comparatively short lifetime Middlesbrough has been transformed and with so many well known landmarks having gone since the 1950s I find myself remembering, in early middle age, the town as it used to be. These two reasons apply to many others, ensuring a continuing interest in Middlesbrough's past.

Exploring these reasons in more detail offers further insight into the reasons for producing another work on Middlesbrough. Consigned to memory are the sight of vast numbers of gas lit streets with their seemingly endless rows of terraced houses which were part of my first impressions of Middlesbrough. From an early age I walked through cobbled streets with my father on damp cold Saturday afternoons as we hurried from Ayresome Park to the United Bus Station. Much of this scene has now gone to be replaced by bright new shopping centres and a modern bus station. The site of the house where my grandparents once lived has, like many others, been replaced by a long stay car park.

Nowadays new shopping centres with their accompanying car parks dominate the scene. Like many others looking for clues about the past, I have discovered the world my grandparents knew submerged under a long stay car park.

Middlesbrough, once an exemplar of Victorian commercial enterprise, has changed completely since the Second World War, especially the town centre where many buildings have been demolished as part of a progressive urban regeneration. Although the physical infrastructure may have gone the spirit of the town most certainly has not been diminished. Regeneration is everywhere, creating historical interest in Middlesbrough in its wake. Paradoxically the demolition of many of the town's older buildings has created for some the mythology that the past is a better place. Cherished memories seen from the security of the present don't always consider the discomfort of life in less accommodating times. For others this may not be the case. Many older people have fond recollections of the close community spirit that existed in the town, something not always so prevalent in new suburban housing estates. For others, visual histories of the town allow a view of places that would have been a familiar part of the daily life of their forbears. Whatever the reason, pictures of the past will always hold a purpose and interest.

It is not surprising then that the idea for this book was originally an attempt to find something about the Middlesbrough my grandparents must have known, particularly the period up to 1945 - that year was an appropriate watershed as it was then that the regeneration we are familiar with today really began. It was in 1982 that I wrote the first major draft of this text. I was then busy with other writing, including books on Billingham and Cleveland, so the work on Middlesbrough was put to one side to be revived in the mid 1980s. It was a delayed resurrection that only came after seven years working on an unfinished doctoral thesis. During that time other new material came to light and this was able to be used when I revised the text again in the mid 1990s.

This work then is the result. I have aimed to give something of the feel of life in Middlesbrough from the perspective of the ordinary person who resided in the town. As I have already stated I have tried wherever possible to avoid a structured chronological approach. For those who lived through those days which are mentioned I can only hope that a few pleasant memories are stirred. For those readers who like myself can only look back at the past with curiosity, I hope this work satisfies but not satiates that interest.

I would like to apologise for any mistakes in the text. In my opinion the real expert is the reader, certainly they will let me know of any errors I have made. Last, but by no means least, I must thank my wife Andrea who with her bright presence and sharp appreciation has surely made writing this book easier than it would have been. Andrea, together with my daughter Lara, has also had to tolerate me while working on this book - not always an easy task as they will tell you! A final note of thanks to Lawrie Coulthard, part of the Cellnet team at the Riverside Stadium, Middlesbrough for his constant encouragement.

Paul Menzies
September 1997

One
The Early Days

As we approach the two hundredth anniversary of the founding of Middlesbrough, a classic example of 'Herculean industrial growth', it is very difficult to portray in our minds the isolated farmhouse on the banks of the River Tees that was once Middlesbrough. A lack of visual evidence does not help historians in this task, with precious few images remaining of the farmhouse nor of the town's early days other than paintings and line drawings. Section One looks at some of the evidence of those early days in the new town.

This picture completed by Joseph Dodshon in 1832, from a point which would be today on Snowdon Road, gives us an impression of what early Middlesbrough looked like. Clearly consisting in 1832 of little more than a few houses along with the original Middlesbrough Farmhouse, the picture provides an idea of how this building stood on a small hill close to the river. A topographical outline is provided through a numerical annotation which was inserted later. Some points to note (with their numerical reference) are the Middlesbrough Farm (1), Ship Inn (6), Commercial Street (11), Stockton Street (12), Dacre Street (13) (this goes up towards the old farm), West Street (14) and Suffield Street (15). One other annotation to note is the town's first 'Lock-up' (9)!

Having purchased 213 hectares of land stretching from the River Tees to the present Southfield Road, the Owners of the Middlesbrough Estate (the consortium of Quaker businessmen behind the modern town) then employed Richard Otley to plan out their town. Otley used a grid plan, setting out 125 plots for sale. This map extract from the mid 1850s clearly shows Otley's symmetrical plan with its central market square along with a number of main streets leading from this. (Reproduced from the 1856 Ordnance Survey map)

A close up of the Ship Inn with Stockton Street behind. In front of the Ship Inn is the stell (stream) which marked the western extent of the new settlement at that time. Next to the Ship Inn are the houses along Stockton Street.

Middlesbrough's rapid development is evident in this image, an extract from a painting completed in the mid 1840s. This view looks across the Tees from Port Clarence towards Commercial Street and behind that, the first town centre. Coal staithes have been erected along the river bank, enabling coal to be tipped from waggons into waiting colliers. Behind them is the entrance to North Street that went up to the Market Square. Mid-centre is the original Exchange building, with its Grecian portico. Constructed in 1837, this later became the Exchange Hotel, the Council Offices, then finally in 1881, the Customs House. Behind the Exchange, St Hilda's church can be seen, consecrated on 25 September 1840, while to the right is Stockton Street, still the western perimeter of the development at that time. A steam ship sails down the river and in the distance the corn mill that once stood in Mill Street is visible. Mill Street ran between Wellington Street and Sussex Street, virtually the southern perimeter of the town before the 1850s.

Several older settlements existed close to Middlesbrough such as Newport, shown here c. 1908, with an unidentified group of people standing outside. A 1618 plan shows a ferry crossing in existence at Newport. The main building there was Newport House, a family home and granary, built for the Hustler family of Acklam, probably in the seventeenth century. This was used by ships, unable to navigate the River Tees up to Stockton, to load and unload their goods. Despite encroaching urban development the settlement at Newport remained relatively self contained until the mid-nineteenth century with a public house, a small number of cottages and a few service establishments including a butcher.

This extract from the 1895 Ordnance Survey sheet (6 inch) gives a good idea of the geographical relationship of Newport, Ayresome and Old Linthorpe villages. It also allows us to locate with some precision some of the images included in this first section. (Reproduced from the 1895 Ordnance Survey map)

The final traces of old Newport disappeared in the early 1930s when the construction of the Newport Bridge necessitated the demolition of the remaining cottages from the old hamlet. The front of Newport House is in the distance, partially obscured by an outbuilding, while the end of one of the buildings in old Newport is also just visible. (See also p. 93.)

Close to Newport was the hamlet of Ayresome, a diminutive collection of cottages which, like Newport, was once part of the township of Linthorpe. The cottages at Ayresome, close to the left turning, stood at a point where today Ayresome Green Lane and Ayresome Lane meet. The lady shown mid-centre is walking towards what is today West Lane.

Ayresome Grange Farmhouse, shown here *c.* 1895, was once the family home of William Strangeways, 'Gentleman'. It stood on Ayresome Green Lane just beyond Blue Hall (see the next picture) almost opposite today's vehicular entrance to the General Hospital. It is uncertain how old it is although a seventeenth century map shows a building here. Both Ayresome and the Ayresome Grange Farm appear on the 1895 Ordnance Survey map of the area, but by 1913 the latter has gone due to continued local development.

This view, from the west of Blue Hall, provides an interesting rural image of Old Linthorpe (the prefix 'Old' avoids confusion with New Linthorpe, part of the southwards expansion of Middlesbrough). Behind is Ayresome Green Lane, while just visible to the right is the road to Old Linthorpe (now Burlam Road). A few people in Victorian dress have come out to pose for the photographer. No exact date can be assigned to the photograph, but Blue Hall was demolished around 1870, so it is probably mid-Victorian. It is uncertain when Blue Hall was built but architectural details (crossed mullions and transoms of many windows) suggest a late seventeenth century building (see Waterson and Meadows, *Lost Houses of York and the North Riding*). This is corroborated by the inclusion of Blue Hall, 'The Seat of Peter Consett Gent' in Samuel Buck's 'Yorkshire Sketchbook' in 1720 and on a 1730 plan of Middlesbrough and Acklam.

14

Situated west of Blue Hall, Old Linthorpe village like Newport was another self-contained settlement which predates Middlesbrough by many centuries. This nineteenth century drawing shows some of the few simple cottages in the village which stood along what is today Burlam Road.

The 'township' of Old Linthorpe spread beyond the cottages shown above. The cottages shown here stood in St Barnabas Road until they were demolished in 1935.

Oldgate Farm, seen here from the south *c.* 1902, stood in the open countryside close to the lane which went from Middlesbrough to Old Linthorpe. The name Oldgate has lived on in a sense, as the name given to the Workhouse built in the fields of the farm was 'Holgate' and in turn the West End at Ayresome Park (also built in the fields of Oldgate Farm), became the 'Holgate End'. Behind the farm can be seen some of the housing development along Ayresome Street.

Another view of Oldgate Farm, this time from the west, probably during its demolition in 1902. The 1895 Ordnance Survey map (see p. 12) shows that the farm was sited along what is now Kensington Road just to the east of the eventual site of Ayresome Park.

Two
Old Middlesbrough

Section Two looks at 'Old Middlesbrough', the original town, or as it is known locally, 'Over The Border'. This phrase probably derived from when a new branch line, constructed along a route south of the town to serve the new Middlesbrough docks, effectively placed a 'Border' between the original town and the subsequent development to the south. The original town was planned for a population of 5,000 people, a figure quickly exceeded resulting in a need for new housing. As the railway line to the south effectively hemmed in the old town until around 1850, builders began to build houses in yards and courts between the streets of the original plan. These were inadequate from the beginning resulting in many parts of 'Over The Border' quickly declining into slum housing.

South Street was originally the main route south from the old town via the lane to Old Linthorpe. This view, c. 1908, provides a detailed image of Edwardian Middlesbrough with its busy pavements, shops and overflow of stalls from the Market Place. One of the town's best known shop proprietors, Amos Hinton, had his first shop in South Street. Arriving in 1862 as an apprentice to John Birks a greengrocer, Hinton later bought his master out. He opened in Albert Road one of the town's best known shops and played a not inconsiderable part in the civic life of Middlesbrough becoming Mayor by 1886. In the distance the Market Hall and the first Town Hall are all visible, while the 'Foreign Money Exchange' building on the corner of Henry Street, reminds us of the town's links with shipping. Beyond this building is Suffield Street which had a public house, The Fleece and The Globe on each corner. Pottage's, a drapers shop, close to the corner of Garbutt Street can also be seen. Feversham Street is just visible at the end of the next block of buildings.

This close up of South Street, *c.* 1909, again shows daily life in Edwardian Middlesbrough, with people standing around talking, others walking along, while a solitary policeman standing in front of Seaton's market stall, carefully views the scene.

The Market Place, at the end of South Street, was dominated by the Market House and the Town Hall built in 1846. The Talbot Hotel is on the right. Nicknamed 'Sackers' or 'The Dog', the Talbot is where Middlesbrough Football Club is reputed to have been formed in February 1876. As ever, a photographer's presence causes some people to stop and stare, although the cyclist and the two small children playing on the corner appear not to be bothered. St Hilda's church is in the distance.

Taken in the Market Place, this provides a better view of the Market Hall and the Town Hall. It was in this building that W. E. Gladstone, Chancellor of the Exchequer, was received amidst much celebration and civic pride on Thursday 9 October 1862, following his visit to Bolckow and Vaughan's Iron Works. A Mayoral Address was followed by a banquet for 200 guests in the nearby Oddfellows Hall (on the corner of Bridge Street West and Albert Street) before Gladstone went to stay overnight at Upleatham Hall, home of the Earl of Zetland.

Beyond this busy market scene, c. 1907, there is a more extensive view of St Hilda's church seen here from the south. A dinner celebrated the opening of the first public market in Middlesbrough on 12 December 1840. The market proved to be so popular that it was expanded in 1856 with a vegetable market opening on the corner of East Street in 1861. The building housing the vegetable market and the unusual bell tower which stood outside, can both be seen here. A butchers' market opened in 1865 on the corner of West Street, on the opposite side of the Market Place.

Older residents will recall Middlesbrough Market remaining open at the height of its popularity until almost midnight. Its shooting galleries, roundabouts and other amusements made the market an essential part of Saturday evening for many people as can be seen in this view, *c.* 1910, with its crowded market stalls. In the foreground a crowd of people have congregated possibly around a travelling salesman, whose cajoling is bringing roars of laughter to the crowds. Familiar names of traders included Walter Bishop, Richardson's, J.D. Lane, Whitfield's, Garbutt's, Bella Miller and Hartley's. Although Middlesbrough Market closed in 1959 it has been resurrected, and is now held near the Hill Street Centre. North Street, sloping down towards the river with the old Exchange building, is also just visible in the distance.

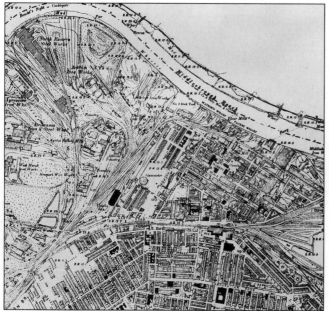

This map shows in detail the Market Place and some of the nearby streets. Several of the infamous courts and yards that contained some of the town's most squalid housing along with several of many public houses in the old town can also be seen. (Reproduced from the 1895 Ordnance Survey map)

Market Square, viewed here from the west, c. 1909, was often the subject of calls to move it to another location, especially after the town spilled south across the railway line. In 1883 a deputation brought to the Council a petition signed by over 2,000 people requesting the market be moved to the more popular district between Newport Road and Linthorpe Road. Then again in the late 1930s there were calls to place it close to the Grange Road area but once more this failed to bring any change of location.

St Hilda's church, here shown c. 1908, stood in the north east corner of the Market Place, having been erected mainly through public subscription in 1840 on land donated by the Owners of the Middlesbrough Estate. Originally the church had a capacity for 600 people but this was later increased to 900 people when a gallery was added in 1861. The church was demolished in 1969. Also visible, just in front of the vegetable market, is a roundabout, one of the amusements often to be found in the Market Place during the years when it was a place of entertainment for many people.

Surprisingly this oxen pulling a cart down Durham Street, having just crossed the river by the Transporter Bridge, is not from the Victorian era but is from the early 1930s. It seems to be attracting attention from people walking by although why oxen are being used is not known.

Sussex Street was once on the southern perimeter of the town and it petered out into a lane to Old Linthorpe. When the branch line to the new Middlesbrough Docks was opened, a small halt and platform were built in 1841 close to where the lane crossed the railway. The railway crossing is shown here around 1908 with the Crown Hotel in Bridge Street West beyond the railway and the corner of Station Street in the immediate foreground.

As Middlesbrough's population increased beyond its original expectations, Otley's precise grid pattern of streets became choked by dense house building with infilling occurring on a massive scale. Dark gloomy courtyards and small streets with no adequate ventilation, sewerage arrangements or water supply were constructed, resulting in 'slum' housing. Despite a series of cholera and typhoid epidemics and a number of commissioned reports across the latter half of the nineteenth century, change was slow to occur. The First World War held back until 1919 a 1914 municipal house building programme, and only in 1927, following a obligatory survey by Middlesbrough Corporation of inadequate housing, was action taken to rectify the problems of slum housing in the old town. An Improvement Scheme centred around Dacre Street demolished houses in that area followed by further slum clearance in the Nile Street area in the early 1930s. This photograph shows the Nile Street area in 1934 during the demolition programme, with the Town Hall on Albert Road in the distance.

Property owners provided strong opposition to the slum clearance programmes. Many considered good property as well as bad was being destroyed and that the proposed compensation was inadequate. However the medical evidence overwhelmingly favoured the clearances. In the late 1930s a report from the Medical Officer of Health stated that the death rate in the old town north of the railway exceeded the whole of the Borough by 50%; while deaths in the old town from tuberculosis were double the rate for the Borough. Evidence of these conditions is shown here as two Middlesbrough Councillors watch an inhabitant of Robinson's Yard, off Lower East Street, using a communal water tap in 1933. According to contemporary newspaper reports there were several yards where water taps and lavatories each served several families living in houses infested by vermin.

This picture of Port Clarence in 1933 shows the close proximity which many local people lived to industry, in this case an iron and steel works. Like the disease ridden courtyards in Old Middlesbrough this brought many problems for these residents with pollution and poor housing leading to inadequate living conditions. Nevertheless the spirit of the woman hanging out clean washing to dry in this polluted atmosphere has to be commended.

Opposite: Looking towards the corner of Newport Road and the Newport Bridge approach road, c. 1935. The corner of Orwell Street is in the immediate foreground, while in the distance past Mills Street, is the partially visible spire of St Cuthbert's church, the only building in this view still standing today. Built at the end of the nineteenth century to help with the expanding parish of St Paul's, it has a very different function today as a sports centre. Opposite the church, underneath the advertisement for Percy's Stores, is the road to Newport Bridge. The opening of the Newport Bridge in 1934 initiated a new lease of commercial life to Newport Road bringing the area to the notice of many people using the new road link to Billingham for the first time. Contemporary reports claimed that increased business meant that by the mid 1930s over two hundred shops were trading along the one mile length of Newport Road. Older residents especially will recall shops such as Doberman's, Eaton's and Sam's.

Three

Newport Road to Corporation Road

After 1850, with the arrival of the iron industry along the banks of River Tees close to Newport, a second phase of urban expansion began in Middlesbrough, as the town finally spread south of the railway. Under the control of the Owners of the Middlesbrough Estate, a major period of building now occurred to provide new housing and created a central road system still familiar today. Based on a regular pattern the two main routes south, Linthorpe Road and Albert Road, criss-crossed three routes running west to east, Corporation Road, Grange Road and Borough Road, all bordered to the east by Marton Road. To the west the turnpike to Stockton (Newport Road) had no convenient connections to the town's road system. This land, originally owned by the Hustler family, was developed separately around a new area of housing, North Acklam, as the Ironmasters' District between Newport and Middlesbrough became established. Echoes of this can be seen in modern times as only in recent years has the town had an adequate east-west route with the A66 development. Physical expansion of the town also brought corporate development with a Royal Charter of Incorporation in 1853 bringing the appointment of a Mayor and Corporation. The next three Sections look at some of the areas which were part of this post 1850 development starting with two of the best known roads, Newport Road and Corporation Road.

A Middlesbrough Corporation bus, the 'O' service, on its way to North Ormesby from Norton, passes the new roundabout at the approach to the Newport Bridge in the mid 1930s. The roundabout caused quite a lot of controversy because it was considered too big! Borough Engineer at that time, Cecil Gorman, replied that as the roundabout was there to stop overtaking and slow down the traffic he was more than satisfied with it.

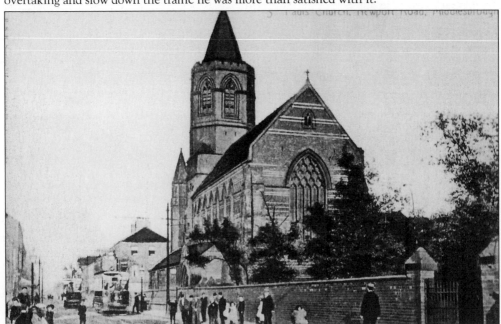

St Paul's church, which stood on the corner of Newport Road and St Paul's Road, was consecrated in 1871 when it was called 'St Paul's, North Acklam' - a reminder of the link between this part of town and the Hustler family. Bombed during World War Two, St Paul's lost its steeple in 1963 and was demolished in 1967. Two tram cars, one with passengers in the exposed upper deck pass each other, while the dress of the many other figures gives ample evidence of fashions at the time of this view from around 1906.

After the new turnpike road linking Middlesbrough to Stockton, via Newport, was opened in 1857, an acre of land owned by the Hustler family adjacent to the road and named 'Long Plantation', was donated along with a financial contribution for the purposes of building a new hospital, the Middlesbrough Infirmary. The new hospital was more convenient for the treatment of casualties from the nearby Ironmasters' District and replaced the town's Cottage Hospital which had opened in 1859. The Infirmary was opened by H.W.F. Bolckow on 5 June 1864 having cost £7,865 to construct. Although various extensions have been added since, the hospital is still instantly recognisable today. Its future is uncertain though with the town's proposed centralisation of its hospital services to South Cleveland Hospital due to occur in the next few years. Incidentally during 1857 to 1866 there was a toll bar close to the Infirmary site.

Beyond the Cannon Street area, Newport Road curves towards Corporation Road, *c.* 1910. Dale Street is on the left and the old Cleveland Hall on the right. Built in 1871 as auction and display rooms, the Cleveland Hall soon became a social club. Thomas Thompson rented the Hall from 1908 and started Middlesbrough's first cinema there until it closed in April 1930. Six years later the Cleveland Hall was demolished to make way for the new United Bus Station.

Many people will recognise this view of the United Bus Station shortly after it opened in 1937, as it was unchanged until its recent modernisation. Contemporary newspaper reports approved of the new terminus, calling it a great asset for the community, bringing more people into this area of the town and brightening up a 'very gloomy area'. Before the United Bus Company opened their new bus station in Newport Road, the company's vehicles had used the town's only main bus terminus in the Exchange Square.

Beyond the bus station a well known landmark for many local people was 'Newhouse Corner', shown here *c.* 1922. John Newhouse came to Middlesbrough in 1865 setting up as a draper. Success brought a move to larger shop in Albert Road, followed by premises on this prominent site in Newport Road. Opposite Newhouse's on the corner of Linthorpe Road is Manfield's Boots Store, while beyond Newhouse's, on the corner of Hill Street, was the United Presbyterian church. Built in 1865, the final service in the church took place on 27 July 1919. It then became the Scala Cinema but despite being popular this too eventually closed on 8 April 1961 when it was demolished to make way for shops. The name Hill Street lives on as the name of one of two main shopping centres in the town.

Looking in the opposite direction to the previous photograph, we look down to Corporation Road as a bus passes Binns on its way to the new bus station in the mid 1930s. Originally opening in 1923, Binns quickly proved a success and a major programme of extension to the store was completed in 1937. Interestingly the tram lines can still be seen although trams had disappeared from Middlesbrough in 1934.

Only a short distance from where the previous photograph was taken Newport Road meets Corporation Road. This busy pre 1914 scene shows a No. 36 tram passing the Wesleyan chapel, with the Corporation Hotel, Town Hall, Empire Theatre and industrial skyline further in the distance.

The sign on the lamp standard warns tram drivers 'Cross Roads - Drive Slowly' but the difficulties of tram drivers are easy to appreciate looking at this picture, c. 1906. One group of schoolchildren wait outside the Wesleyan chapel to cross the road yet another boy has decided not to look, take his chance and dash across. We hope he made it! Beyond the boy is the Institute building which stood between the Wesleyan chapel and the Corporation Hotel.

Moving on eastwards down Corporation Road, it is crossed next by Albert Road. This view taken from that corner, c. 1905, shows how the skyline is dominated by the then recently opened Empire Palace of Varieties with its terracotta coloured brickwork. A tram approaches the Town Hall, while in the distance two tall chimneys are a constant reminder of nearby industry.

The Empire Palace of Varieties, shown here c. 1907, has a history of distinction, stretching back to the days when the music hall was the most popular entertainment in the land. Built on a site previously used by circus shows, the Empire had six private boxes and other seating for more than one thousand people. Many of the world's greatest stars have graced the stage of the Empire since the opening night on 13 March 1899, including Charlie Chaplin, Stan Laurel, Gracie Fields, George Formby, Will Hay, W.C. Fields and probably the greatest of them all, Marie Lloyd. In October 1937 Sir Harry Lauder, returning to Middlesbrough after an absence of thirty-three years, paid tribute to the 'spirited nature' of the audiences at the Empire. Although the Empire has had a more uncertain history in recent times it has recently undergone a worthy restoration. I was fortunate to visit it and even in a time of disrepair the theatre still had a wonderful atmosphere with many wonderful interior decorative features visible. One other point is that the building on the left with the bow fronted windows is the Central Hotel.

Looking back towards town along Corporation Road, a horse pulled wagon and distant tram approach from Newport, *c.* 1912. The corner of Peacock Street is on the left, with Martin's Garage further along. Opposite, the shop can be seen which belonged to Robert Dennis, a provisions merchant. As always, the presence of the photographer arouses the curiosity of children - note the two boys with what appears to be a pram in the middle of the road. They could not know their place in posterity would be secure, a moment of time preserved forever.

Four

Going Down
Linthorpe Road

Linthorpe Road is probably the best known thoroughfare in the town and also one of the oldest. One of only two exit routes from the new town of Middlesbrough in 1830, the road to Old Linthorpe is known to have existed in the early seventeenth century. Linthorpe Road, which broadly followed this route, was a significant road in the post 1850 development of Middlesbrough south of the railway, becoming a prominent commercial and trade route and remains so today.

A very busy scene indeed at the junction of three of Middlesbrough's best known roads, Linthorpe Road, Newport Road (on the left) and Corporation Road, c. 1908. In the distance at the northern end of Linthorpe Road is the Leeds Hotel with the Middlesbrough to Redcar railway line beyond that. In the foreground is the King's Head Hotel which stood on the site which is today occupied by Debenham's store. Two cyclists, complete with their straw boater hats, ride cross the road junction. Hats were fashionable in Edwardian Middlesbrough as almost all of the figures are wearing one.

Opposite the King's Head Hotel was Collingwood & Son Goldsmiths whose shop had been on the corner of Linthorpe Road and Corporation Road since 1886. Like many of the town's prominent shops, Collingwood's was a story of entrepreneurial purpose. Matthew George Collingwood opened a jeweller's shop in the old Market Place in 1855, moving to South Street, then Cleveland Terrace before moving to this site. A policeman looks towards the camera while in the immediate foreground a boy with his errand basket stands on the corner of Linthorpe Road outside the Wesleyan chapel. Beyond Collingwood's are some of the shops on the northern part of Linthorpe Road.

Opposite: Once again the camera brings the immediate locality to a halt as people pose for their own moment in posterity. The boys in the foreground are standing outside the White Horse Hotel while the Masham Hotel is on the next block of buildings on the corner of Vaughan Street. This view is a postcard bearing the town's crest and its motto 'Erimus' (We shall be).

Another bustling scene on the corner of Newport Road and Linthorpe Road. Beyond the King's Head Hotel is the Cleveland Book Store on the corner of Johnson Street while men are on ladders at the White House premises. In the distance is the turret of the Leeds Hotel, a familiar landmark for people before the hotel was destroyed during an air raid on 26 July 1942.

Linthorpe Road, Middlesbrough.

Another view of the northern end of Linthorpe Road, *c.* 1912, from a point which today would be opposite the C & A department store. A horse-drawn cart waits patiently underneath Poole's clock at 1.35 p.m., with other business premises such as Hood's and Robinson's also visible.

Opposite: This scene looks southwards down Linthorpe Road from the junction with Newport Road and Corporation Road. On the immediate right is Manfield's Boot Stores while on the left is the Wesleyan chapel, a building held in high esteem by the people of the town and fondly nicknamed 'Big Wesley'. Originally bought in 1860 for £2,000, the site was then on the southern outskirts of the town. Opening on 20 September 1863, the chapel also housed a school but this closed in 1908 being replaced by a large hall. This was built over the shops in Corporation Road becoming a popular venue for lectures and local concerts. Many residents married in 'Big Wesley'. John and Elsie Lindbergh told me that when they were married there in 1925, the wedding took place at 8 a.m. and the guests walked there from their home in nearby Fry Street! Sadly the spiritual had to give way to the secular and 'Big Wesley' was sold in 1953 to be demolished when the British Home Stores department store was built.

At the northern end of Linthorpe Road was Wilson Street. In the middle of the row of buildings on the right is the Hippodrome Palace of Varieties shortly after it opened in August 1906. Before construction began, a night time exhumation of the bodies was necessary because it was the site of a Quaker burial ground. Florrie Ford, famous music hall star of the day topped the bill on the first night but the Hippodrome subsequently had a chequered history. Fierce competition forced closure in 1908 before it was re-opened shortly afterwards, this time showing films in addition to the variety bill. The first full length 'talkie' seen in Middlesbrough, *The Singing Fool* with Al Jolson was shown here in August 1929.

Opposite 'Big Wesley' from 1923 was Binns department store. As can be seen here from this 1937 view the shop was greatly extended, including an extra 75 feet of show windows. The extension enlarged the whole store to 17,225 square feet and there were four floors and a basement.

The splendour of the new store seen here was short lived as it was burnt down in a spectacular blaze on 27 March 1942. Although the fire was not caused by enemy action, it was so fierce that it lasted more than six hours, involved more than forty-eight fire appliances and completely destroyed the store. The outer shell of the building was left and for a while was so dangerous that pedestrians were not even allowed to walk on the same side as the store.

Beyond the Binns store in Linthorpe Road, crowds walk past the three ornate lanterns hanging down over the frontage of the Imperial Hotel, c. 1910. Directly opposite the Imperial Hotel was Wesley Street while the King's Head Hotel (now Debenham's store) and the northern end of Linthorpe Road can be seen in the distance.

As it went southwards, Linthorpe Road was joined by several roads which no longer exist such as Newton Street, seen here c. 1910, behind the lady crossing the road. Richardson's (jewellers) is on the corner of Newton Street while Fosters stood in the distance on the corner of Fallows Street. Newton Street later gave its name to Newton Mall, a thoroughfare in today's Cleveland Centre. Behind the boy in the striped blazer are the premises of Wilson's (boot maker) in Gilkes Street. Today these premises are Dixons.

LINTHORPE ROAD, MIDDLESBROUGH.

The familiar grid layout is found in the development which occurred further south down Linthorpe Road, as illustrated in this view taken close to the junction with Grange Road, c. 1910. Roads criss-crossed Linthorpe Road all the way down as shown here. On the right is Norton Street while opposite is Davison Street with Red Cross House (a chemists) on the corner. It is also possible to see further in the distance, the Cafe Royal, a popular place for many people in the days before the First World War.

Five

Albert Road and Exchange Square

Albert Road, like Linthorpe Road, linked pre 1850 Middlesbrough with the more substantial post 1850 development to the south. Commencing at the Exchange Buildings, Albert Road terminated at the Middlesbrough High School. At its northern limit, Exchange Place linked Albert Road to Queen's Square in the old town via the Albert Railway Bridge. Several admirable buildings, architectural symbols of Middlesbrough's commercial endeavour, graced Albert Road, but none were more splendid than the Exchange Building and the Town Hall. The Exchange Building opened in 1868 while the Town Hall opened in 1889, a glorious confirmation of the town's increased importance. Both replaced counterparts in the old town and both made a statement about just how far Middlesbrough had developed commercially during the Victorian period. These then are the themes of Section Five.

A single pony and trap stand outside Victoria Park at 2.30 p.m. one afternoon in Edwardian Middlesbrough with the scene dominated by the pseudo Gothic style Town Hall and its clock tower of 870 feet.

The Town Hall and Municipal Buildings were of course the centre of Middlesbrough's civic affairs. Many important events took place there ranging from visits by the famous to official announcements of war, elections or royal events. One such occasion is shown here with the proclamation of the accession of George V being read out by the Mayor of Middlesbrough, Sir Samuel Sadler on 22 March 1911.

Two trams trundle slowly along Albert Road and three girls look at the camera from the corner of Grange Road West, *c.* 1910. Again the Town Hall dominates the horizon. The power to construct the new Town Hall was part of the Improvement Act of 1877, when the Corporation bought a piece of land from the Owners of the Middlesbrough Estate. First prize in a competition for the submission of plans in 1882, was won by G.G. Hoskins and the foundation stone was laid amidst great pomp and ceremony on 24 October 1883 by the Mayor of Middlesbrough, Isaac Fidler.

The Town Hall, shown here *c.* 1908, cost £130,000 to build. The official opening on Wednesday 23 January 1889 was by the Prince and Princess of Wales. The Royal Party arrived by train in Middlesbrough just after 12.10 p.m., then accompanied by Mayor Raylton Dixon and other dignitaries they proceeded to the Town Hall, via the old town, Linthorpe Road, Grange Road and Albert Road, the whole route bedecked with decorations. Princess Alexandra set the clock going using an electric button, the first time Royalty (in a public capacity at least) had performed such a duty using electricity. The Prince was presented with a memento, a key of gold and Cleveland steel. Dunning Street and Russell Street can also be seen behind the bandstand.

Victoria Square, next to the Town Hall, has for many years been important as a place of pleasure for people in the town. Previously used as a cattle market, a circus, a cycle track and as a skating rink during the winter, Victoria Square, complete with ornamental garden and bandstand, was opened by Colonel S.A. Sadler on 12 July 1901. Music was provided by the Coldstream Guards. The Square soon became popular, as this view from around 1906 illustrates.

VICTORIA PARK, &
CARNEGIE LIBRARY, MIDDLESBROUGH.

By 1912 seats had been presented for the 'sole use of old people' and as this view, c. 1913, shows they soon became popular. The statue of John Vaughan, previously in Exchange Place (see p. 49), was later moved to Victoria Square on 23 October 1914 joining the statue of another famous citizen of the town, Sir Samuel Sadler, whose statue had been placed in Victoria Square on 21 June 1913. The town's new library is shown in the distance.

The Carnegie Library, shown here from south west shortly after its opening by Alderman Amos Hinton on 8 May 1912, replaced the Free Library housed in rooms at the Town Hall on the corner of Albert Road and Russell Street. A generous donation of £15,000 from Andrew Carnegie in January 1908 enabled the new library to be built on land donated by Sir Hugh Bell in Grange Road and Amos Hinton in Dunning Street.

The junction of Corporation Road and Albert Road close to the Town Hall, c. 1925. Many of the windows of the Corporation Hotel are on the immediate left, while on Corporation Road is the shop where Amos Hinton firmly established his position as a leading shopkeeper within the town with Freeman Hardy and Willis opposite. Hinton's shop was between 1858 to 1875 the site of Dr William Grieves' grammar school attended by both boarders and day pupils.

The No. 51 tram, which terminated at the railway bridge and station, approaches the northern end of Albert Road, *c.* 1907. The tram is passing Newhouse's with its white awnings giving shade to the front of the shop. The business was here from 1890 until 1912 when it moved to a more prominent site on Newport Road (see p. 28). In the distance a horse and cart wait patiently at the junction with Wilson Street while another horse and cart is being led by a man towards the photographer.

A closer view of the business which belonged to John Newhouse, *c.* 1913. Initially it was a drapers shop but with development the shop sold a much wider range of goods. Next to Newhouse's is Wilson Street and then the Exchange Building, surely one of Middlesbrough's finest examples of Victorian architecture before it was demolished in the 1980s.

The west front of the Exchange Building and a view down Wilson Street towards Exchange Square, c. 1906. As often seems to be the case a tram (No. 17 this time) is also in the picture! Construction of the Exchange Building cost the Middlesbrough Exchange Building Co. Ltd £28,000 despite a 130 foot tower not even being built due to a lack of money.

A different perspective, looking from the station across Exchange Place, shows the Exchange Building from both the north and west. Albert Road and Marton Road are also visible. It seems fitting that the statue of John Vaughan overlooks the Exchange Building because with his partner Henry Bolckow, he installed the town's first blast furnace in 1851 initiating the second more substantial phase of Middlesbrough's commercial development. Other ironmasters followed these pioneers and the town quickly gained national prominence within the iron industry.

After opening on 29 July 1868, the Exchange played a leading part in Middlesbrough's commercial life. The Iron Market was held here each Tuesday and Friday fixing price levels, facilitating the buying and selling of iron as well as other commodities. The unveiling of John Vaughan's statue by Sir J.W. Pease on 29 September 1884 in Exchange Place, close to Middlesbrough's commercial centre, confirms Vaughan's important role in Middlesbrough's development. John Vaughan had also lived in Cleveland Square beyond the other side of the railway bridge until October 1858 when he moved to Gunnergate Hall. In 1868 Vaughan died in London. Vaughan's statue was later moved to Victoria Square on 23 October 1914.

Across Exchange Place is Middlesbrough Railway Station. Built in 1877, this replaced a smaller station which had been built on the same site in 1847. As with the other public buildings constructed at this time, it was a bold attempt at Victorian grandeur reflecting the increasing importance of Middlesbrough. Unfortunately the station's fine roof was badly damaged during an air raid on 3 August 1942, during which seven people were killed. A row of horse drawn cabs stand close to the Albert Bridge. Incidentally the cab drivers hut shown close to the cabs was later moved to Albert Park.

At the east end of the Exchange Building was Exchange Square, well-known as a bus terminal until recent years. The statue of H.W.F. Bolckow, a prominent figure in Middlesbrough's development, is enclosed by an octagonal fence around which sit a group of boys. The building behind the carriages is the post office. Middlesbrough didn't get its own post office until the 1840s. After moving to Marton Road in 1869, this building opened on 17 September 1879. Also in view is the Freemasons' Hall which held its first meeting on 12 January 1861, having cost £150 for the site and £838 for the building and furniture.

A horse and cart waits patiently at the end of the Post Office Chambers, *c*. 1912. Zetland Place is just visible on the left. Bolckow's statue, unveiled by Lord Cavendish on 6 October 1881 during the town's 50th Jubilee celebrations, represented a fitting memorial to a man prominent in Middlesbrough's commercial development. Born in Sulten, Germany in 1806, Bolckow came to work in Newcastle in 1827, amassing a fortune of over £40,000 and forming a partnership with John Vaughan to set up in business at Stockton. When no suitable site was available at Stockton they came to Middlesbrough at the invitation of Joseph Pease. After they bought six acres of land in Commercial Street for £1,800 on 18 May 1840 to establish an iron foundry, Bolckow and Vaughan became the driving force behind the development of the iron industry in the post 1850s era. Bolckow was a considerable benefactor of the town in many other ways, including financing the purchase of land for Albert Park in 1868.

A boy runs across the new Exchange Bus Station shown here shortly after it opened in 1925. When the Exchange was developed as a new bus station, Bolckow's statue was moved to Albert Park. Motor buses from several companies used the bus station including United and one of the company's vehicles is shown here bound for Redcar. Although the town still had trams running until 1934 they didn't use this terminus. Behind the bus terminus is Wilson Street on the left and the Exchange Building.

This view of the Exchange Bus Station taken in the winter of 1928/29 shows the thick fog that would often enshroud the town turning day into night. Being in close proximity to so much industry meant that dense fog like this was a common occurrence.

After the Middlesbrough Tramways Committee took control of the Exchange Bus Station on 21 January 1930 they quickly decided the site required further development which necessitated demolishing the bus station built in 1925. This view, taken from upstairs in the Exchange Building, shows the site in May 1930 surrounded by hoardings ready to be knocked down.

The new bus station shown here opened on 6 March 1931. As Middlesbrough expanded with a great deal of new housing being built away from the centre of the town more services were needed to serve the new communities. Examples of this include the new Brambles Farm housing estate constructed in the late 1920s which had a new service from 31 October 1931.

In 1938, during the demolition of buildings in Marton Road near the post office and Jordison's the printers, the old St John's school house was discovered. Revd Adam Smith, a vicar of St John's in Marton Road (then still called New Road), wished to provide education and found this site for St John's School which opened on 16 January 1860. At one time the school had nearly five hundred pupils who paid 2d per week and it was also used as a Sunday School. When the school was replaced by the expanding printers, the old school house was left standing, a unique link with the first period of development south of the railway line. One link with the school remaining today is School Croft, the street which still exists behind the old post office building.

Six

A Glimpse of
the Suburbs

Middlesbrough received its Royal Charter of Incorporation as a Municipal Borough in 1853, becoming a County Borough in 1889. Once the old town had expanded south of the railway after 1850 the development gathered pace. Eventually, through a number of Boundary Extension Acts in 1858, 1866, 1874, 1913 and 1931, many neighbouring communities including Linthorpe, Newport, Ayresome, Acklam, Marton and Ormesby were officially included in the boundaries of Middlesbrough.

Development continued to the south along Linthorpe Road and this group of buildings on the left near to St George's church are situated close to the junction with Southfield Road and Princes Road, c. 1908.

A No. 52 tram passes the Linthorpe Post and Telegraph Office on its route to the ferry landing in the old town, *c.* 1907. New Linthorpe was established along the southern end of Linthorpe Road to the east of the much older agricultural village of Linthorpe. Originally built to provide housing for workers from the nearby brick works, New Linthorpe became part of the expansion southwards of Middlesbrough.

A No. 57 tram awaits passengers in The Avenue, Linthorpe, *c.* 1907. The tree lined suburban roads of sizeable Victorian villas in New Linthorpe were generally favoured by those who had the desire and the means to live away from the centre of the town. Even though the road structure in this area had been laid out much earlier, the development of this area was still ongoing after 1900 due to the local economy slowing down as a result of the great depression in the iron trade from 1873 to 1896.

54

Swatter's Carr is mentioned as early as 1618 on John Gibbon's plan of the area and the farm of that name stood on the corner of Southfield Road and Linthorpe Road until the late nineteenth century. This view, possibly from around 1870, probably looks south as the mill on Acklam Green Lane and new housing development south of Middlesbrough may be the buildings in the far distance. Several shows (including the Cleveland Agricultural Society annual show in 1879), fairs and circus shows were held on the Swatter's Carr land before it was gradually sold off to building developers in the latter part of the nineteenth century.

The Grand Opera House built at a cost of £38,000, on the site of the Swatter's Carr Farm, was opened by Samuel Sadler MP on 7 December 1903. Many famous artists appeared here including Charlie Chaplin (in 1912 with Fred Karno), Gracie Fields and Jack Buchanan. The Opera House closed on 21 June 1930, later to be re-opened on 31 March 1931 as the Gaumont Cinema (see p. 91).

Albert Park, the gift of Henry Bolckow to the people of Middlesbrough, was opened on Tuesday 11 August 1868 by Prince Arthur of Connaught. The Prince had arrived the day before, staying at Bolckow's home, Marton Hall. On the day of the opening, having visited Eston Mines, the Prince was met at the Toll Bar on Marton Road, travelling to Albert Park through the old town and then up Linthorpe Road to Albert Park. Following the opening ceremony, there was a public banquet in the Exchange Hall and then a ball at Marton Hall. These elegant entrance gates shown here around 1907 had been purchased by Bolckow at an exhibition in York in 1867, while the clock was presented by Alderman Thomas Sanderson in 1900.

Albert Park quickly became a very popular place for the people of Middlesbrough. Here crowds of people gather around the bandstand listening to a summer concert around 1907. Built in 1890, the bandstand survived until June 1962. Other attractions included a maze (similar to that at Hampton Court) which opened on 10 August 1894.

For many years one of the main attractions in Albert Park were the three boating lakes, the Upper, Lower and North Lakes. Although only the Lower Lake, shown here *c.* 1910, survives, all three were obviously a very popular place of enjoyment for the people of the town. Incidentally the fencing had to be placed around the lake due to several people falling in and drowning.

In 1872 a large tree, which had been salvaged from the River Tees close to the furnaces of Samuelson and Company, went on display near to the entrance of Albert Park. The tree was thought to be part of a forest which once stood at Newport.

New Linthorpe became quite a fashionable place for middle class people from Middlesbrough to live (see p. 54). Sycamore Road, shown here around 1908, shows the type of 'Edwardian villa' typically found in the area. These houses were in direct contrast to the more basic housing found closer to the town, especially 'Over the Border' within the original nineteenth century settlement.

One of the Imperial Tramways Company buses en route from the Exchange to Cambridge Road via Abingdon Road, c. 1925. The vehicle, a Bristol single decker bus, was one of several which were used on routes within the town. Little protection is given to the driver during bad weather.

Seven
Down by the Riverside

There is little question of the significance of the River Tees in the development of Middlesbrough. When the new coal staithes were constructed at Port Darlington in 1829 to provide the coal trade with a new shipping point, the River Tees assumed an importance which continues into the modern era. Much of the trade using the River Tees was highly specialised reflecting the industries along the land adjacent to the river; thus following the demise of the coal trade the development of the iron industry saw a steady growth in the import and export of goods associated with the industry. Section Seven looks at some images associated with the river.

RIVER TEES, FROZEN OVER, CHRISTMAS DAY 1860 TO MARCH 1861.

A group of men stand on the ice around their ship when the River Tees reputedly froze over from December 1860 to March 1861. I have not been able to verify this but Thomas Richmond records there was certainly a very cold period in January 1861 during which the port of Stockton was closed for almost a month. Previously the Tees was reputed to have frozen over for most of January and February 1780 and from 24 January until 25 February 1784. During the latter cold spell a sheep was roasted on the river at Portrack.

This view looking across to Port Clarence, *c.* 1907, shows the proximity of industry to the river. Several masted ships, including a four masted vessel moored near the staithes at Port Clarence, can be seen. The chimneys of the Bell Brothers' Clarence Iron Works are visible in the distance.

The *Erimus* ferry boat seen at the Middlesbrough landing, *c.* 1906, was one of a number of ferry boats which operated between the town and Port Clarence. Built by Raylton Dixon and Company and launched on 15 September 1888, the boat was licensed to carry 927 passengers. *Erimus* operated until the Transporter was opened when it was sold for £725 to Messrs Pollock, Brown of Southampton along with its sister ferry boat the *Hugh Bell*.

Several sailing vessels are moored in front of the Clock Tower and the row of terraced houses which stood along Dock Street, c. 1908. Middlesbrough Dock was built on marshland east of the original town when it was realised that an enclosed dock with a constant water level would be more beneficial than the coal staithes built at Port Darlington. Designed by Sir William Cubitt, the dock opened on 12 May 1842. Ten coal drops were served by a fan of railway lines from the Dock Branch, an extension from the original Stockton and Darlington line to Port Darlington. When the dock opened the enclosed water area was 3.6 hectares but further extensions in 1869, 1886 and 1902 extended this to 10.1 hectares with the dock containing approximately 2,134 metres of quayage.

This is an unusual view because it shows not only the dock but also one of the partially constructed towers of the Transporter Bridge at Port Clarence, c. 1911. Some of the masts from sailing ships moored in the river can also be seen along with buildings at Port Clarence.

The sailing ship *The Caradoc* docked in Middlesbrough, *c.* 1908. The number of sailing ships using the river fell steadily throughout the nineteenth century and by 1890 only 33% of ships cleared on the Tees were sailing ships, a figure which declined to only 14% by 1913.

A general increase in the size of ships and a need to handle other cargoes after the decline in the shipment of coal, led to the reshaping by 1902 of Middlesbrough Dock from its original configuration, including the building of new quays. Two ships stand in one of these around 1912. Behind them is the swing bridge across the dock entrance and alongside the ships further refurbishment of the dock is visible including the installation of more cranes to increase the capacity for the loading and unloading of goods.

Many of the iron works which brought Middlesbrough international renown were situated between Newport and the Transporter Bridge, an area which became known as the Ironmasters' District. Newport Iron Works, shown here around 1912, located close to the site of the modern day Newport Bridge, was also close to the Cannon Street area of housing. Newport Iron Works were taken over by Dorman Long in 1917 during the First World War but eventually closed in 1930.

A group of men look across to the Acklam Blast Furnace, c. 1912, which was situated at the northern end of the Ironmasters' District, close to the old town.

MIDDLESBROUGH FERRYBOAT.   Nº711.

Another view of the *Erimus* ferry boat, *c*. 1907, as it makes its way across the river with the Middlesbrough ferry landing on the right.

No book about Middlesbrough would be complete without the town's most famous structure - The Transporter Bridge. Built at a cost of £87,000, the Transporter Bridge was opened with much celebration on 17 October 1911 by Prince Arthur of Connaught. Staying at Rounton Grange as a guest of Sir Hugh Bell, the Prince also visited Albert Park, opened forty-three years earlier by his father and then went on to Kirby School.

Eight
Preparing For War

As with many other towns the preparations for war were evident in 1938 during the Munich crisis. While Neville Chamberlain was doing his best during his visits to Germany to appease Hitler, Middlesbrough was responding to the Air Raid Precautions Act of 1937 requiring Local Authorities to prepare schemes for ensuring the safety of their citizens. The first A.R.P. committee meeting took place on 25 February 1938. In April an appeal was made in the town for seven to ten thousand volunteers able to serve in the event of air attacks. Preparation for war was now officially under way.

During the Munich Crisis of September 1938, a feeling that war was imminent swept across the country and patriotism was generally high. Local newspapers reported that after a group of volunteers and the A.R.P. committee finished assembling 132,000 gas masks at 11 p.m. on Wednesday 28 September 1938, they burst into cheering and spontaneous singing of the National Anthem. Sandbags were placed around important buildings including the Town Hall Crypt which was to act in the case of an emergency as the 'nerve centre' controlling the town's resources. Workmen are shown here placing sandbags around the Town Hall in a view looking down Albert Road, towards Hinton's shop in Corporation Road.

By April 1939 air raid shelters were being issued. Mrs J.C. Williams (shown here) of 1, Hutton Road was the first person in Middlesbrough to receive their Anderson Shelter. However, not every citizen responded with urgency in erecting their shelter. By the end of July 1939, local newspapers reported that out of 5,750 Anderson shelters already delivered less than one third had actually been erected by the recipients.

Players from Middlesbrough Football Club reported back for pre-season training on 5 August 1939. Lining up before a pre-season game at Ayresome Park in aid of the FA Jubilee Fund in August 1939 against Sunderland are: Back Row: Henry Fowler, Duncan McKenzie, Jackie Milne, Dave Cumming, Billy Forrest, Bobby Stuart. Front Row: Mickey Fenton, Benny Yorston, Bobby Baxter, Wilf Mannion and Cliff Chadwick. Middlesbrough lost their first two games of the season, 2-0 at Aston Villa and 4-1 at Liverpool. In what was to be their final league game before war began, Middlesbrough drew 2-2 with Stoke City at Ayresome Park before just over 12,000 fans. On 23 September 1939 it was announced that season tickets would be returned to fans.

Part of the preparations for war included A.R.P. Practice Schemes when the town underwent a practice air raid to test the precautions. One practice testing the effect of the blackout took place on 18 April 1939. Members of the A.R.P. Committee, including those seen here, from left to right: Councillor Sir W.H. Crosthwaite (chairman), Alderman E. Spence and Councillor H. French, toured the area in a fire engine travelling to the top of Ormesby Bank to obtain a view of the whole district before they declared the whole event a 'huge success'.

The effects of war were not just felt locally. When Jewish refugees poured out of Germany, this group of children came to stay in Middlesbrough during February 1939, at a house in Linthorpe, No. 5, The Avenue. I have no further details about this particular group or why they came to this particular house but I have often been curious as to their eventual fate.

Obviously this was a time for propaganda photographs but even allowing for this the invincible spirit of Middlesbrough's residents is clearly shown in this picture from June 1940 showing the people of Clyde Street in their street shelter which they have made 'just like home' by adding furniture and decorations. These included the Union Jack flags which are just visible hanging from the roof of the shelter

It had been decided in June 1939 that seven air raid shelters would be erected in Victoria Square for employees from the municipal buildings. As can be seen from this photograph, taken in October 1939, the Square was already being transformed. The Town Hall can be seen complete with its sandbags while the statue of Sir Samuel Sadler is also visible.

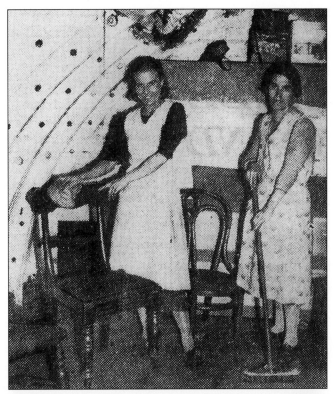

Another scene portraying the indomitable British spirit. A resident of the town, Mrs Banks (on the right) is helping the war effort in September 1940 through her work as the voluntary caretaker of the street shelter in Barritt Street, close to Southfield Road. Her duties included keeping the shelter tidy and looking after the comfort of those who used it. Mrs Banks is being ably assisted by a neighbour in her task.

Public air raid shelters sprang up all over the town and this one is being constructed by workmen in September 1939 on the Clairville Recreation Ground. One point to note is how deep these shelters were sunk into the ground.

As war became more likely many soldiers were involved in preparatory exercises. These two photographs are taken during an exercise in April 1939 when approximately 100 men of the 107th 'A' Field Company Royal Engineers (SA) from the Middlesbrough Bright Street Drill Hall practised being attacked by aeroplanes along the road from North Ormesby to Ormesby village. Imaginary gas bombs were dropped on the troops by members of the 608th Squadron Air Force of Thornaby, with the event being watched by a large crowd of spectators. The troops are seen here marching through Brambles Farm on their way to the exercise.

The troops go into action south of Brambles Farm using a Lewis Gun. It is interesting to note that traffic appears to be continuing normally along the road to Ormesby village, almost oblivious to the military activity.

Nine

Best Days of our Lives

The first school erected in Middlesbrough, in Stockton Street in 1837, catered for over 200 children. Several schools opened in the town before the passing of the 1870 Education Act, many ran by churches. Many schools which have opened since 1870 have now become history; thus the names of schools such as Denmark Street, St Paul's, Fleetham Street, East Street, Marton Grove, Boundary Road, Hugh Bell and Middlesbrough High have all gone. Some are remembered here along with a few other miscellaneous memories of school life within the town.

Empire Day was once celebrated with great ceremony in schools with many older citizens able to remember scenes like this. These are children at Newport School in 1931, marching with pride past the Union Jack. Newport School on the corner of Anne Street and Victoria Street, opened in 1884, being one of the schools catering for the increasing numbers of children in the expanding population of Middlesbrough in the late nineteenth century.

These infants at St Hilda's Infants School, situated on Innes Street at the northern end of Snowden Road, are smiling because they have been allowed to wear their bathing costumes during a heat wave in July 1934. It is interesting to wonder if anybody recognises themselves or perhaps a friend or family member, although children from this group will now be pensioners.

This happy group are from the St Hilda's Sunday School, pictured in 1934 outside the School House, Market Square prior to their annual trip, probably to Redcar. The influence of the church was still powerful in 1930s Middlesbrough with many children attending Sunday School throughout their childhood.

New housing estates built after the First World War on the perimeter of the town meant new schools were needed. One estate, Brambles Farm, had by April 1932 more than 500 houses and over 1,000 children under sixteen, many of whom were causing congestion attending neighbouring schools in North Ormesby and Cargo Fleet. Eight acres of land were purchased and a crowd of onlookers watch the foundation stone of the school being laid by J.W. Brown (Chairman of the Education Committee) in May 1934. Brambles Farm School opened almost a year later on 29 April 1935.

Whinney Banks, like Brambles Farm, needed a new school to provide education for a new local population. The Infant Department at Whinney Banks School had been in use since 1 September 1937, although the school was not officially opened until 13 July 1938. This photograph shows one child, on the school's first day in 1937, who decided helping the workmen who were still constructing the adjoining buildings was more fun than school.

This view shows some of the first children to attend the Infant Department at Whinney Banks School in 1937. The schools built in the 1930s were vastly superior to some of the Victorian school buildings in the town, many of which, with their dark high walled classrooms and concrete playgrounds, compared badly with these grass playing field sites.

One school which opened following the 1870 Education Act was Middlesbrough High School. When it first opened it was in Grange Road, with another house being used for the Girls High School from 11 August 1874, with an aim to improve pupils for the Cambridge Local Examinations at thirteen. This view is taken from the rear of the school around 1907.

When increasing numbers of pupils at the High School meant that a new site was needed, J.W. Pease offered a site at the southern end of Albert Road. The school opened here on 15 January 1877. During these early days the area in front of the school (eventually to be occupied by Constantine College and later Teesside Polytechnic) was allotments. The High School moved out to the Prissick Base in September 1959 and today only the tower of the High School and part of the wing joining it survive.

This group of pupils from Middlesbrough High School are enjoying some time at a school camp at Hawnby, near Helmsley in August 1937. Unfortunately the name of the master and the boys are unknown. Perhaps someone reading this will be able to help?

Another school built during the development southwards of the town was Kirby School. Four acres of land on the corner of Orchard Road were purchased by the Education Authority in June 1908 and the school, named after R. L. Kirby, a chairman of the Education Committee, opened on 17 October 1911 when Prince Arthur of Connaught performed the ceremony after opening the Transporter Bridge. One of the longest serving members of staff at Kirby School was Miss M. McCombie, headmistress from 1916 to 1943.

Acklam Hall, family seat of the Hustlers from the late seventeenth century was sold to Middlesbrough Corporation on 3 September 1929 for £11,500. In 1929 Middlesbrough Boys High School took 570 pupils; this meant that two classes were having to use the school hall as a form room. Acklam Hall School was seen as the answer to this problem. First some alterations had to be made and they are shown here close to completion in August 1935, only weeks before the first 231 pupils started. Approximately twelve rooms were big enough for classrooms but some of the smaller bedrooms had to have partition walls taken down. Initially the old dining hall was to be the art room, a gymnasium would be built in the Hall's old garage and stables were to be converted into science rooms. A number of new buildings were also constructed. When Acklam Hall School opened, the High School continued to take pupils from north of a line running from Newport, Ayresome Street, Park Road North and Longlands, the others going to the new school.

The official opening of Acklam Hall school took place on 23 July 1936. One link with the Hustler family was retained as a bell from the Hall, cast in 1815 and used on the Acklam Estate to denote the start and finish of the working day, was cleaned up, mounted and used to indicate the start and finish of lessons. This photograph was taken at Speech Day a year later in July 1937, always a day which attracted many local dignitaries. Those involved here include, the Mayor and Mayoress of both Stockton and Thornaby, Professor F. Smith from Leeds University and the headteacher of Acklam School R. Gill.

This time the photograph is of some of the pupils arriving at Acklam Hall School for the Speech Day in June 1939, the last one before war began. Nearly sixty years later many of the boys will now be aged seventy or more. I wonder how many will recognise themselves?

The Hugh Bell Schools which faced Victoria Square, on the site occupied today by the Teesside Law Courts, were two of the best known in the town. The original site was purchased on 11 September 1889 for £3,375 from the Owners of the Middlesbrough Estate and the school was opened as the Grange Road Schools on 2 May 1892 by Alderman (Sir) T. Hugh Bell. The schools became known as the Hugh Bell Schools on 6 December 1898.

This is a group of pupils from the Hugh Bell Girls School in July 1937, enjoying their sports day. Hugh Bell Schools were one of several schools who used the Vicarage Sports Ground at North Ormesby, previously the home of Middlesbrough Cricket Club. The site behind the vicarage had been acquired by the Education Committee in 1932 for the use of schoolchildren. Today the vicarage is the Old Vic public house.

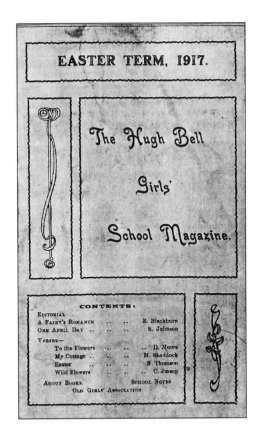

The front cover from the Hugh Bell Girls School magazine published at Easter 1917, a time when the life of the town was dominated by news of the First World War.

CAPTAIN COOK MEMORIAL SCHOOLS, MARTON.

The outlying areas of Middlesbrough, such as the village of Marton, provided their own education facilities for local children. Here, pupils are standing outside the Captain Cook School in Marton in the early part of the twentieth century.

War also dominated the late 1930s. In 1937, during the Spanish Civil War, twenty Basque refugees from Bilbao were brought over to stay at Hutton Hall, after permission was given by Sir Alfred Pease. Aged between seven and fifteen the refugees were invited over by the Middlesbrough Branch of the National Joint Committee of Spanish Relief, a key figure of which was Mrs Ruth Pennyman of Ormesby Hall. In this photograph from July 1937, the refugees are being visited by Mrs Ruth Pennyman of Ormesby Hall and Sir Alfred Pease along with the Mayor and Mayoress of Redcar.

Five of the Basque refugees are seen here walking through the grounds of Hutton Hall in July 1937, obviously happy to be away from the conflict going on in their country. I am unsure about what happened to them. Perhaps a reader may know.

80

Ten

Those Special Days

This section is a fairly random selection of some of the memorable days that occurred in the town before the Second World War. There is no real basis for the choice of events - indeed they have been driven more by the availability of the material rather than any distinct criteria. The only aim in choosing this cross section of events has been to include events which feature a variety of people who lived in the town.

Mineral Street celebrates during the Coronation of 1937, within a year it was demolished as part of the slum clearance programme, north of the railway. The street ran parallel to Cleveland Street linking Lower Gosford Street and Lower Feversham Street. Crowded with houses, very few people probably remember it now but this photograph is evidence that the residents who lived there were determined not to be left out of the Coronation party.

Two years before the Coronation another major celebration took place - the Silver Jubilee of George V. Looking down Albert Road across Corporation Road, towards Victoria Square, Hugh Bell School is just visible beyond the bus. The Town Hall, adorned with decorations, exemplified the town's festive mood. Another highlight was a Thanksgiving Service at the Albert Park war memorial, with a procession over two miles long of societies and groups ranging from the Fire Brigade to the Girl Guides, marching there from Newport Road via Glebe Road, Gresham Road and Linthorpe Road. They joined civic dignitaries and a crowd of thousands in what local newspapers described as a 'solemn service'.

As well as the official celebrations many streets in Middlesbrough organised their own events. One in Ernest Street (which linked Newport Road and Union Street), included a tableau of past monarchs. Here two young 'Jack Tars' salute Queen Victoria, played by Mrs C. Willett.

Another place where the residents had done themselves proud was Grange Street, 'over the border' just off Lower Feversham Street. Although one of the poorer parts of the town, mums and children proudly pose in front of the large Union Jack painted on the wall at the end of the street. Even the cobblestones have been whitewashed.

The children from the town being presented with Jubilee medals from teachers at one of the Middlesbrough schools.

Nelson Street in the Cannon Street area linked Denmark Street School to Newport Road. Here on Jubilee Day a large crowd of people have gathered in the street to enjoy a community celebration. Once again the elaborate decorations are easily visible, many houses being festooned with Union Jacks or other decorations.

Crowds are gathered outside the United Methodist church in Grange Road East (today this is the site of the Police Station) in November 1931 to pay their final respects to Sir Joseph Calvert, a former Mayor of Middlesbrough and Director of Education. On 7 November 1919 Sir Joseph had been made an Honorary Freeman of Middlesbrough for his work as a Town Councillor for twenty-one years and for his civic services during the First World War.

Middlesbrough celebrated its Golden Jubilee a year late, on 6 October 1881, because of the high unemployment in the town at that time. This meant that its centenary was also celebrated a year late in 1931. From 5 July a week long series of events were staged, including planting trees in Stewart's Park, civic processions, dances, and band concerts. One special event on Friday 10 July was a gathering of the town's schoolchildren at Ayresome Park. The Mayor, H.D. Levick made a presentation to each school followed by parades of children. In this view the civic party are walking in front of the North Stand at Ayresome Park with the Mayor in the centre of the gathering.

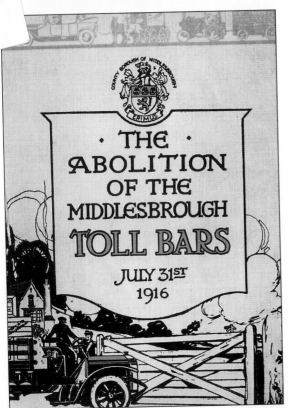

Toll bars had been erected during the nineteenth century on all privately owned roads. Various toll bars had already been abolished but in 1914 an Act was passed abolishing the five which remained within the Middlesbrough area as from 31 July 1916. This is the front of the commemorative programme produced to mark the occasion.

North Ormesby Road toll bar, which was jointly owned by J.S. Pennyman and the Owners of the Middlesbrough Estate, with a horse drawn vehicle stopping to pay the toll, c. 1916. The toll bar stood close to the railway crossing at North Ormesby.

The toll bar furthest south was on Cargo Fleet Lane, close to Ormesby village. This view shows the toll bar cottage on Cargo Fleet Lane looking towards Cargo Fleet, then only a country lane. The toll bar was owned by Lord Furness.

Lord Furness owned another toll bar on Cargo Fleet Lane close to Cargo Fleet village at the junction with South Bank Road. The question of toll bars had caused Middlesbrough Council problems for several years and there was widespread relief when they were finally demolished. Compensation was paid to those who had a financial interest in the toll bars.

One of the highlights in the 1930s for employees of Binns department store, Middlesbrough was the annual inter-store sports. This group of employees in 1937 at Middlesbrough Station are off to this event held that year at Sunderland. An interesting point to note here is that being pre-war, the station roof is still in place and is just visible.

Many of the town's working people looked forward to the annual summer trip. This group were members of the National Union of Tailors and Garment Workers waiting at Middlesbrough Station to make their outing to Windermere. Once again, a point to note here is that in 1937 it was possible to travel direct to the Lake District from Middlesbrough using the Darlington to Kirkby Stephen route over Stainmore.

In the days of accessible travel it is easy to forget that before World War Two poor or elderly people living in the town often only left Middlesbrough on pleasure trips once a year. Many only did this by going on annual outings provided for them. Ready to enjoy their special day, an outing to Carlton in August 1933, are Mrs Sarah Hammond aged ninety-two and Mr A. Bullock aged eighty-six, the two oldest guests of the Newport Old Aged Pensioners.

The Newport Workingmen's Institute took a party of women and children on an outing to Redcar in August 1933. They are waiting here on the old Newport Station for the arrival of special trains to take them. For many of these children this would be their only visit to the seaside that year as many families suffered from the ravages of poverty during the high unemployment which occurred during the 1930s.

There were two main tram routes in Middlesbrough; from Norton Green to North Ormesby and from the Transporter Bridge to Linthorpe. The system was owned by Imperial Tramways until 1921 when it was taken over by Middlesbrough Corporation and the Stockton and Thornaby Joint Tramway Committee. By 1929 Stockton wanted to scrap trams but Middlesbrough didn't agree. After lengthy negotiations it was agreed to withdraw the Norton service and on 31 December 1931 the last tram made its final journey from North Ormesby to Norton Green, before being replaced by motor buses. The Linthorpe to Transporter service survived until 9 June 1934 when at 11 p.m. tram No. 103 made the final journey from the Transporter. Despite no official farewell service many hundreds of people came to see the event, crowding on to the tram as it pulled into the Linthorpe terminus for the final time. The tram cars were sold - some to Southend and Stockport while others went to Birmingham to be used as hen runs.

Once the tram service had finished, the job began to dismantle the overhead equipment and workmen are shown doing this in Albert Road in June 1934. Ironically one of the 'new' motor buses that had taken over from the trams can just be seen on the edge of the picture.

THE
GAUMONT PALACE,
MIDDLESBROUGH
THE WONDER THEATRE OF THE NORTH-EAST.

DELIGHTFUL SURROUNDINGS,
PERFECT LIGHTING,
GIGANTIC SCREEN.

ALL COMEDY PROGRAMME—
TOM WALLS
IN
ON APPROVAL
ALSO—
MICKEY MOUSE
Delightful Humour.

LESLIE JAMES
ON THE
MIGHTY COMPTON ORGAN.

MATINEES: 6d & 1/-; EVENING, 6d, 1/-, & 1/6.

Continuous Performance.—6 p.m. to .0.30.
Matinees: 2 to 4.30.

Saturdays Continuous from 2 p.m. to .0.45.
No Booking of Seats.
Luxurious Waiting Rooms.

Middlesbrough Opera House on the corner of Southfield Road and Linthorpe Road, which closed in June 1930, re-opened on Monday 30 March 1931 as the Gaumont Cinema. This is the advertisement that appeared for that first week in the local newspapers. The cinema claimed it was the most up to date in the town. It had to be because competition was fierce with many cinemas open in Middlesbrough by 1931.

The opening of the Gaumont Cinema, performed by the Mayor and Mayoress of Middlesbrough, was one of the events of 1931. Mayoress, Mrs Levick, receives a bouquet of flowers from a young boy, with the surname of Merson, watched by crowds of people who had assembled close to the cinema on Linthorpe Road.

91

In 1934 Middlesbrough finally got its second bridge across the River Tees when the new Tees Bridge opened at Newport. Approval for the new bridge was given in 1924 but further lengthy negotiations carried on throughout the 1920s so the foundation stone wasn't laid until 1932.

This is a view from the top of the new bridge looking towards Middles-brough along the approach road from Newport a few days before the official opening in February 1934. In the distance smoke rises from the chimneys of the endless houses on either side of Newport Road.

To allow construction of the new bridge, sixty-one houses were demolished and seventy families rehoused on the new Whinney Banks estate. This view, and the one below, show some of these buildings that were demolished; some were part of the village of old Newport.

Workmen lay the track for a crane to operate from prior to the demolition of the old cottages at Newport. In the distance is Newport House, once used by the Hustler family as a granary.

The new Tees (Newport) Bridge was opened on 28 February 1934 by the Duke and Duchess of York (now the Queen Mother). Arriving on the previous day, the royal couple stayed at Wynyard Park and visited the ICI factory at Billingham before their engagement at Newport. Here are some pupils from Kirby School waiting to greet the Duke and Duchess.

Following the civic and religious proceeding in which the Bishop of Durham gave a benediction, the Duke declared the bridge open and then walked across it with the Duchess and civic officials. The Duke is accompanied here by the Mayor of Middlesbrough, Councillor Alfred Cooper.

The Duke also inspected the Durham Light Infantry and they are seen here marching up the approach road to the bridge watched by a large crowd. In the background, the new bridge is in the raised position waiting for the Duke to lower it during the opening ceremony.

Despite the construction of the new bridge, bathers still swam in the river at Newport. This group pictured in the heart wave of July 1934 seem to be enjoying taking a cooling dip.

Col. Wharton

Lord Irwin

Lord Feversham

Lord Zetland

Sir Alfred Pease

Lord Furness

Lord Gisborough

Lord Bolton

Sir Philip Cunlitte-Lister

Col G.R Lane-Fo

WELL-KNOWN FIGURES in the hunting and agricultural world who will play important parts at the Great Yorkshire Show, to be held in Middlesbrough on July 11, 12, and 13.

One of the highlights in the history of Middlesbrough during the 1930s was the honour of staging the 93rd Great Yorkshire Show on 11, 12 and 13 July 1933. Previous to this Middlesbrough had hosted the show in 1906 and 1892. This caricature shows some of the officials who were responsible in organising the event. Great excitement was caused by the whole event and for several days before the show began the leading local newspaper, the *Evening Gazette*, carried information on the events as well as other advertisements for people to stay when they were visiting the area. The show was actually held on a 100 acre field at the Prissick Farm, one of the largest sites that the show had been held on at that time.

As well as a wide range of farm stock at the show and agricultural activities like the judging of sheep shown here, there were also lots of trade stands with many of the town's leading businesses in attendance. Trade Stand No. 194 was Dickson and Benson, No. 17 was Tower House with demonstrations of rug making, No. 13 was Binns and No. 30 was Uptons. Local dairy merchants, Bruntons were giving a free pint of milk to all who attended their Trade Stand. At Stand No. 185, Hardy and Company erected a small seaside bungalow in which to demonstrate their furnishings. Regular bus services served the show. One went from Queen's Square via Linthorpe Road and Marton Burn Road while the other left the Royal Exchange and travelled via Marton Road, both were one minutes walk from the Railway Station and the fare was 3d (1p). A three course lunch at the Binns stand was 1/6d (7p) and at stand No. 77 the *Evening Gazette* churned out up to date editions of their paper using the latest in printing technology.

One of the other events was the awarding of a Gold Cup to Middlesbrough if they could beat the record attendance previously set at Leeds. The local media whipped up enthusiasm for this with notices saying 'help your town win the cup and attend the show' and daily attendances were reported in the press. Finally the attendance for the show was announced as being 52,232 an improvement of 10,000 upon 1906 when it had been held on land at Park Vale Road and 3,000 more than at Leeds, enough to give Middlesbrough the Gold Cup. A final tribute to the town was made by Show Secretary A.S. Cavers who was reported as saying that although the popular image of the town was one of being smoky and grimy, it was in his opinion one of the finest settings they had ever had for the show with such a marvellous large site framed by the nearby hills bathed in sunshine.

When Middlesbrough Golf Club's golf course in Linthorpe, near Salter Gill Farm, was threatened by building work it was decided to create a new course near Marton. Two farms, Brass Castle and Bonny Grove were purchased in 1936, one of them, Brass Castle, seen here in October 1936, was later converted into the new clubhouse.

The famous veteran golfer, James Braid, one of the greatest golfers of all time and the first man to win five Open Championship titles, was engaged as the designer of the new golf course. During one of his visits in April 1938 to inspect the construction of the course, he was reported as being delighted by its natural beauty. Braid is seen here with the Middlesbrough Golf Club professional, Claude Weastell, J.F. Copeland, H.H. Jones (vice-captain), John Stutt (contractor) and on the extreme right, R.N. Hedley.

Eleven
'Going to the Match?'

For over a century Middlesbrough Football Club has been a part of the sporting life of the town. A demonstration of the people's marked affection for the club was shown in 1995 when crowds flocked to the last game played at Ayresome Park, home of Middlesbrough Football Clubsince 1903. Remaining true to the theme of this book, this Section picks out a few memories from before World War Two, days when 'Boro' were one of the most powerful clubs in football.

A testimony to the excellence of Middlesbrough's new ground at Ayresome Park, opened in 1903, is that two years later the Club was honoured by being awarded an international game on 25 February 1905 (see p. 102) when England and Ireland fought out a 1-1 draw. This view of the ground in February 1914, looking towards the North Stand from the south east corner, featured in the programme for the second international game to be held at Ayresome Park, when England again played Ireland in front of a crowd of 27,439. The game ended 0-0 with local interest focusing on an ex-Middlesbrough High School pupil making his debut for England, George (Geordie) Elliott. In 1914 Elliott was close to his peak and was the country's top goalscorer with 31 goals.

Although they only joined the League in 1899, Middlesbrough were promoted to the First Division in 1902 and during the Edwardian era became established as one of the country's top clubs, going on to achieve in 1914 what is still their highest ever position when they finished third. This photograph taken on 3 September 1910 shows local lad Sam McClure, making his debut at home to Everton, being congratulated by his team mates after scoring the winning goal in front of 17,000 people. Having been unbeaten until 12 November, Middlesbrough moved to within a point of top place after they beat Bradford City 3-2 at Ayresome Park on 17 December. But then disaster struck. Allegations of financial irregularities unsettled the team and after a heavy 5-1 defeat at Blackburn Rovers on Christmas Eve they fell away so badly that they were fortunate not to be relegated.

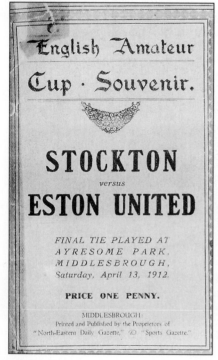

English Amateur
Cup · Souvenir.

STOCKTON
versus
ESTON UNITED

FINAL TIE PLAYED AT
AYRESOME PARK,
MIDDLESBROUGH,
Saturday, April 13, 1912.

PRICE ONE PENNY.

MIDDLESBROUGH:
Printed and Published by the Proprietors of
"North-Eastern Daily Gazette," & "Sports Gazette."

Ayresome Park was also used for other important representative games including the Football League against the Scottish League in February 1912. Two months later the final of the English Amateur Cup between Stockton and Eston United was staged there for the first time. This is the front of the souvenir programme which cost one penny. Today copies of this programme have become a collector's item.

Formed in 1905, Eston United had an remarkable climb to success, gaining national recognition in 1909 when they reached the Amateur Cup Final while still members of the Teesside League. They were admitted to the prestigious Northern League in 1910 and became champions in their first season before appearing in another Amateur Cup Final in 1912. The Eston team includes, standing: Jarvis (trainer), Watson, Roddam, J. Smith, Hill, Housam (captain), Davidson, O'Hara and Barr (assistant trainer). Sitting: Allan, Parsons, W. Smith, Morris and Hollins

In contrast to Eston United their opponents in the 1912 final, top amateur club Stockton, were an experienced team; already Northern League champions in 1898 and 1907. They had also won the Amateur Cup in 1899 and 1903. The 1912 final at Ayresome Park was held in front of 20,479 people and ended in a 1-1 draw. Stockton achieved their third Amateur Cup win the following Thursday when they won the replay 1-0. The Stockton side shown in the photograph included, standing: Stamper, Spence, Evans, Callaghan, Chapman (captain), Veitch, Robson, Callendar and Hornsby. Sitting: Davies, Mascall, Dobinson, Sutherland, Marwood and Frankland.

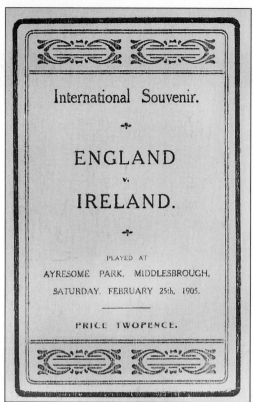

Although programmes from the era before the First World War are now extremely rare some still survive. The front covers shown on pages 102 and 103 are examples of programmes from that period. To celebrate the first international ever played at Ayresome Park in 1905 a souvenir programme was issued. Despite costing twice the usual price, the programme contained only ten pages but did include a photograph of local boy from North Ormesby, Tim Williamson, who was making his debut for England. The game, in front of a crowd of 23,500, was disappointing as it finished 1-1. A further disappointment for home fans was that Williamson had the misfortune to score an own goal for England.

Programmes at this time were officially called Key Cards. This cover is from the game between Middlesbrough Reserves and Seaham Harbour at Ayresome Park on 10 September 1910. Pink in colour and with sixteen pages, it was good value for money. The famous 'Sports Gazette Key Board' which for many years displayed half time scores from other games is shown on the cover. Middlesbrough were the first club to have this innovation, the idea of *Evening Gazette* employee Michael Keegan, when it was erected in 1902 at the Linthorpe Road ground. After the move to Ayresome Park a new Key Board was built where it became a familiar feature. Incidentally the first team drew 1-1 at Sheffield Wednesday on the day this particular Key Card was issued.

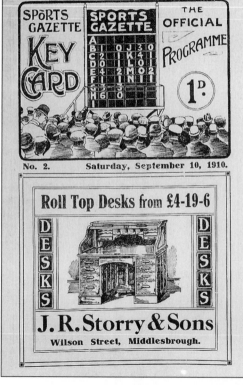

By 1912 the programme had a new front having been increased to contain eighteen pages. This programme for the game against Liverpool, now had a dark blue cover. Apart from advertisements for local businesses and local football notes, the programme contained photographs of Middlesbrough's Mayor and Mayoress, local football officials and caricatures of Liverpool's leading players. An exciting game played in front of a crowd of 11,973 saw Middlesbrough losing 4-3.

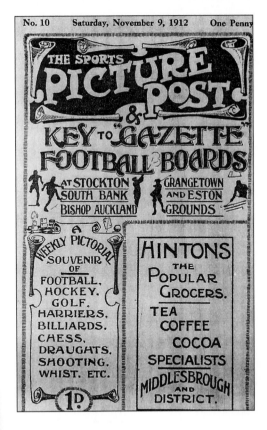

This programme from October 1914 still has a dark blue cover similar to that of the previous one from 1912, but three months into the First World War there is a much more sombre tone inside. Reduced to only twelve pages there is only one photograph – ironically it is of Andrew Jackson, one of the three Middlesbrough players killed in action. The *Evening Gazette*'s announcement about their coverage of the fighting on the front cover is a reminder that war was never far away even at a football game.

Andrew Jackson joined Middlesbrough in 1910 from a Scottish junior side. Making his debut on 3 September 1910 at centre half, he starred in the 1-0 home win against Everton and became a key part of Middlesbrough's team. This was the era when the club had one of their finest teams. In November 1911 they led the First Division ahead of Newcastle United and Sunderland, in second and third places respectively and then finished seventh. A son of a Scottish international, Jackson would almost certainly have achieved international caps. Instead he volunteered to join the army but was killed only a few days after arriving in France. Altogether Jackson made 137 appearances for Middlesbrough scoring three goals. The last of these was against Manchester United only two weeks before his final game for Middlesbrough at Blackburn Rovers. This signed photograph appeared in one of the programmes from that season.

Following the disappointment of being relegated from the First Division in 1924, Middlesbrough finally came back in storming fashion in 1926-27. Although they made a dismal start, losing the first three games, Middlesbrough then proceeded to romp away with the Second Division Championship finishing with a massive points margin of eight points ahead of runners-up, Portsmouth, scoring 122 goals - a Second Division record for many years. One player who probably helped bring about this transformation was a young man signed from Durham City, George Camsell. He first played in the home game against Hull City on 18 September 1926. Middlesbrough won 2-0 and never looked back; neither did Camsell who went on to score 59 goals, then an all-time record for one season. George is shown here in full flight at Ayresome Park against Clapton Orient on 26 February 1927, a game which Middlesbrough won 6-0 with Camsell here scoring one of his two goals. The North Stand can just be seen behind him.

Middlesbrough dominated the Second Division so much that season that they were able to be declared champions before the end of the season. After the final home game, a 5-0 win over Reading, with Camsell getting his eighth hat trick, the crowd spilled on to the pitch and carried captain Billy Birrell shoulder high from the field. Birrell was presented with the Championship Shield by Charles Sutcliffe the President of the Football League. It was probably Birrell's finest moment with Middlesbrough as he left the club six months later and eventually became manager at Chelsea. Camsell went on to become a great servant to club and country. Middlesbrough? Well in typical fashion they came straight back down the following season from the First Division!

Amazingly having been relegated again, Middlesbrough bounced straight back up and won the Second Division in 1928-29! This view of Ayresome Park on 23 March 1929 looks towards the West End, locally known as the 'Workhouse End' during that season. Supporters from more recent times will of course know it as the Holgate End. The photograph features a Boro attack on the Barnsley goal during a 1-0 win in front of a crowd of 17,050. This was one of the last games before a redevelopment of the West End during the close season of 1929.

Promotion in 1929 was celebrated by major ground improvements being announced, mainly to the West End. Old wooden railway sleepers was replaced by concrete terracing complete with crash barriers. As can be seen in this view from June 1929, Ayresome Park is in a state of upheaval as the reconstruction work goes on. Behind the West End stand can be seen buildings of the Holgate Workhouse and the end of Addison Road.

Like their modern day counterparts footballers in 1931 liked to play golf. As part of their preparation for the FA Cup game at home to Bradford City on 14 January 1931, the Middlesbrough team enjoyed a day at Cleveland Golf Course. Ready to drive off here are four of Middlesbrough's stars in the early 1930s, left to right: Jack Jennings, Billy Forrest, George Camsell and Billy Pease. Jennings, later club captain, joined Middlesbrough from Cardiff City in January 1930, while Forrest, signed in 1929, became a stalwart of the side throughout the 1930s. Camsell was already nationally famous for his goalscoring feats and an England international, as was Pease who had been capped for England in February 1927 when still a Second Division player for Middlesbrough. Although they lost to Bradford City, only four weeks later all four players starred in one of Middlesbrough's greatest games, a 5-0 victory over Newcastle at St James' Park.

106

Footballers have always been local heroes, people who commanded a lot of media attention and this was no different more than sixty years ago as is shown in this trio of photographs from June 1931 when Middlesbrough's English international Billy Pease was married. The wedding took place at St Mary's Cathedral in Sussex Street in Old Middlesbrough and the first of the trio shows large crowds gathered as the bridegroom's car arrives at the cathedral.

Billy Pease leaving his car at St Mary's accompanied by his best man, the international swimmer Jack Hatfield one of Middlesbrough's greatest sporting heroes.

The final photograph shows the densely packed crowds outside the cathedral waiting for Billy and his bridegroom to come out, being cheerfully controlled by only two policemen. Apart from the crowd containing men with their flat caps and women with shawls around them this picture could easily have been from the 1990s when similar scenes have occurred many times when members of the Middlesbrough team make a public appearance.

Pre-season training was of course very different during the 1930s for the Middlesbrough players. Here on 1 August 1933 the team line up at Ayresome Park during a break from their first day's training. Welsh international Tom Griffiths, Middlesbrough's captain, leads the line with George Camsell eighth from the right hand side. The man in the background wearing a flat cap is Boro's legendary trainer Charlie Cole who had been with the club since 1912.

One of the most exciting derby games involving Middlesbrough took place on 17 October 1936 when the reigning League Champions Sunderland were the visitors. Over 36,000 people crowded into Ayresome Park and saw Middlesbrough go into a 2-0 lead after seven minutes with goals from Camsell and Coleman. By half time Sunderland had made a remarkable comeback to lead 4-3. Two minutes after half time the goal shown in this photograph from Raich Carter made it 5-3 to Sunderland. A storming rally from Middlesbrough brought another two goals from Camsell and Birkett to end a remarkable game 5-5. One other point of interest is that the photograph shows the goalmouth at the West End with the South Stand behind it. The small stand shown was the former Main Stand at their previous ground in Linthorpe Road, brought with them by the club to Ayresome Park in 1903.

A major redevelopment of Ayresome Park took place in the mid 1930s involving the replacement of the old South Stand with a new grandstand seating 9,000 fans; this picture from the East End shows the work as it nears completion in July 1937. Other work also done at this time included putting for the first time a roof on the West End (Workhouse End).

Not only was the ground being improved in 1937. New players coming to the club strengthened the team and the side of the late 1930s was the strongest since the Edwardian years. A young blonde eighteen-year-old from South Bank St Peter's, Wilf Mannion, signed for Middlesbrough in September 1936. Seen here in pre-season training with George Wardle in August 1937, Wilf had already made his debut in the home game against Portsmouth in January 1937. After scoring in a 2-0 win against Leeds United on 27 December at Ayresome Park he became established in the first team, going on to become one of the greatest players of all time. Even today he is still Middlesbrough's highest capped player having appeared for England on 26 occasions.

The new South Stand was officially opened on 4 September 1937 before the game with Stoke City by Football League President Charles Sutcliffe. Having viewed Ayresome Park on the Saturday morning before the game, Sutcliffe declared it one of the best stadiums in the country. Middlesbrough won 2-1 and here Billy Forrest jumps for the ball just before he put Middlesbrough ahead.

Scorer of the second goal, Mickey Fenton, can be seen in attack as Stoke goalkeeper, Wilkinson punches the ball over his head. Another Middlesbrough player, Benny Yorston, can also be seen. Incidentally the Stoke City team contained a young player who was to play alongside Wilf Mannion in many of his England games - Stanley Matthews. The new South Stand was obviously a great success as record gate receipts were taken during the 1937-38 season and the club made a profit of £8,200 - their second highest in their history.

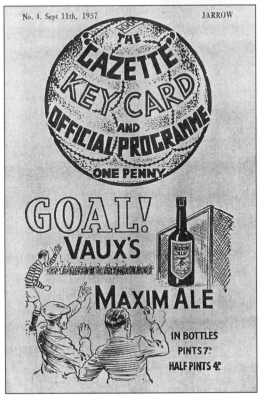

The changing face of the club programme can be seen here in the cover from the one issued for the Reserve team game against Jarrow on 11 September 1937, one week after the opening of the South Stand. The programme now had what can only be described as a very dark red cover but still only costs one penny, the same price as in 1905, thirty years before.

Several Middlesbrough players gained international honours in the 1930s and here George Camsell is about to board the train for London at Middlesbrough railway station, on Tuesday 6 December 1933, as he goes off to play for England against France at Tottenham the following day. Camsell scored two goals in a 4-1 defeat of France maintaining a remarkable scoring record for England which saw him score in every international game he played. Bobby Baxter is on the right.

Bobby Baxter went on to become a Scottish international and is himself being congratulated by the then Middlesbrough Secretary Herbert Glasper after being chosen to captain the Scottish team against England at Hampden Park on 15 April 1939. Standing next to Baxter is Jack Milne who also played for Scotland in that same game and watching on is Wilf Gillow, then Middlesbrough manager.

After a gap of nearly twenty-five years Middlesbrough were again awarded the honour of hosting an England international when on 17 November 1937 Wales were the visitors. The England squad stayed at the Zetland Hotel in Saltburn and this view shows the team relaxing the evening before the game. Playing the snooker shot is Eric Brook (Manchester City) while mid-picture is a very young looking Stanley Matthews. Closest to the camera is Charlie Cole, the Middlesbrough and England trainer, while standing behind him is Stanley Rous.

The game on a damp November afternoon finished as a 2-1 win for England in front of more than 30,000 people. Man of the Match was Stanley Matthews who is shown here (No. 7) as he scores an equalising goal for England at the Workhouse End after Perry had put Wales into the lead after sixteen minutes. The Tottenham player Hall scored the winning goal. As I write this it is nearly sixty years since this game, the last occasion on which Middlesbrough hosted an England international fixture.

One of the most influential figures in Middlesbrough's history, Phil Bach, died aged sixty-four on 30 December 1937 at his home in Philips Avenue, Linthorpe. Proprietor of the Empire Hotel Linthorpe before his death, Bach had a distinguished career in football. First playing for Middlesbrough in the Northern League, he later joined Sunderland during which time he became an England international, being a member of the team that beat Ireland 13-2 at Sunderland in 1899. In his retirement Bach was on the Middlesbrough board for over twenty-four years including two terms as Chairman, being a major figure during the years when the club became established in the First Division. Bach also became an International Selector in 1930. At Middlesbrough's first game after his death, on New Year's Day 1938, two minutes silence was observed by a the 45,854 fans at Ayresome Park - then a record crowd. Here the teams pay their tribute led by the two captains, Bobby Baxter on the left and Raich Carter on the right. Rather appropriately the game happened to be Middlesbrough against Sunderland, two of Bach's former teams and Middlesbrough won 2-1.

Three weeks later Middlesbrough defeated Nottingham Forest in the Fourth Round of the FA Cup 3-1 with goals from Mannion, Camsell and Milne. Middlesbrough now had a strong team with young stars such as Mannion and Hardwick playing alongside experienced players like Camsell and were tipped for honours very soon. However, they crashed out of the Cup 1-0 at York City in the next round. They finished in fifth position in the League and when they improved to fourth in 1939 they were widely regarded as one of the favourites for the title in the 1939-40 season. Unfortunately the war intervened and the team was broken up before it ever reached its full potential. The team for the Forest cup game are pictured here at Middlesbrough railway station. Left to right: Mannion, Birkett, Hardwick, Charlie Cole (trainer), Laking, Forrest, Fenton, Cumming, Baxter, Brown, Martin, Camsell and Milne.

Twelve

Out of Town

Many places such as North Ormesby, Marton or Ormesby, once communities in their own right, have now become part of the town of Middlesbrough. Boundary extensions have seen these places merged into a continuous conurbation, so much so that it is now difficult to see any physical signs they were once distinct places. Included in this final section are a few reminders of these communities at this time.

Captain J.W. Worsley and his son J.S. Pennyman were responsible for the laying out of North Ormesby, selling off land for building after 1852. In association with the Owners of the Middlesbrough Estate they also built a new road from Ormesby to Middlesbrough. The influence of the layout of the planning of neighbouring Middlesbrough can be seen in the grid layout, around a Market Place at the centre, of North Ormesby as it is very similar. Holy Trinity church, seen here on the corner of Charles Street and the Market Place, was consecrated on 26 November 1869. Various extensions to the original building since then have included the addition of a tower in 1880 and clock in 1883.

North Ormesby Hospital, which was situated in Westbourne Grove with accommodation for twenty-five patients, opened on 23 May 1861. The construction was funded by public subscription and for many years workmen voluntarily made subscriptions from their pay to help fund the hospital.

Middlesbrough's new Velodrome at North Ormesby opened in July 1937 when more than 3,500 people watched an exciting programme of cycle races held there. These featured Syd Cozens, the famous English professional sprint champion, against Eddie Smith, one of Australia's top cyclists. Cozens was the overall winner.

At the southern end of North Ormesby, close to where King's Road and Westbourne Grove become Ormesby Road, stood White House Farm. This was for many years the home of George Wilkinson and his family, the last tenants to farm there. Opposite White House Farm there was a brick works. Here members of the Wilkinson family pose for the camera in front of the farm house with their pony and trap harnessed ready to make a journey. The Wilkinsons later moved to Berwick Hills Farm and White House Farm was eventually demolished due to local development. A point of interest is that the Majestic Cinema, opened on 17 December 1938, was built upon land belonging to White House Farm. Today the cinema has now gone with the new Majestic Bingo Centre having replaced it.

George Wilkinson was a proud horse owner and is pictured here at White House Farm with two of his stock in the early part of the century. This view is taken on the other side of the farmhouse shown in the previous photograph.

Councillor J.G. Pallister, an ex Mayor of Middlesbrough, purchased approximately thirty acres of land at North Ormesby in 1925, then donated it to Middlesbrough Corporation to be laid out as a public park. Today Pallister Park has given nearly seventy years of pleasure to local people. This view shows the land in September 1929, before development of the park.

Inevitably as Middlesbrough expanded southwards it absorbed more local farms, the names of which would be forgotten except that they live on as the names of the housing estates built on their land. One example is Brambles Farm, another is Thorntree Farm shown here in 1931 when it was being considered as the proposed site for Middlesbrough's civil aerodrome. This view from the south looks at the front of the farm house with an orchard on either side. Inevitably, as the town crept closer to these farms, vandalism became a problem, so much so that in 1938 Thorntree Farm, then owned by the Middlesbrough Corporation was ordered to be demolished immediately after the building had been completely stripped down to the last window sash by vandals. In the end the aerodrome never materialised and after the Second World War the construction of the Thorntree housing estate began in May 1946.

More new houses were erected after 1945 during a major expansion in Middlesbrough Corporation's housing programme. Another farm, Berwick Hills Farm, was demolished in 1952. This was the home of the same Wilkinson family, who had lived at White House Farm in the late 1930s (see p. 117). Members of the family are shown sitting on their horse and cart in front of the Berwick Hills farm house around 1950.

Another view from Berwick Hills farm shows Raymond Wilkinson making potato rows in the Spring of 1947. The clump of trees in the background were just east of the farm itself.

Although many of the conditions of town houses were undesirable, people lived in squalid conditions in other areas too. This caravan colony, shown here in 1931, was sited between North Ormesby and Cargo Fleet. Ellen Wilkinson, then Labour Member of Parliament for Middlesbrough East and a vigorous champion of the impoverished, made a strong attack on the Housing Committee of Middlesbrough Town Council following her visit to the site. She claimed that people living here should have been given first consideration for the houses in the nearby Brambles Farm housing estate.

The reality of how hard life could be for people working on farms was to be found only a couple of miles from the centre of Middlesbrough. Here in September 1933, a group of potato pickers are hard at work in a field next to Marton Bungalow when despite a long drought there was a good crop in that year.

Having filled their baskets the women then had to fill sacks. It was certainly a very demanding task for them but the women who lived in rural areas had long been accustomed to having to make a contribution to the labour required in the running of a farm.

Marton Bungalow, which stood on the corner of Marton Road and the south side of Ladgate Lane, was a popular place to call for refreshment for many people when they either went for a walk or cycled on a Sunday to Marton village. It was demolished some years ago.

Even in 1935, when this was taken, traffic census was used to monitor the volume of cars on roads in the local area. This census was being completed on Marton Road close to the junction with Ladgate Lane.

Marton, shown here *c.* 1907, was very much a rural village right up until the Second World War. On the left is the old Rudds Arms while houses line the road up to the church just beyond the trees.

One of the events which still took place in the 1930s was the meeting of the Cleveland Hunt at Marton. A large crowd stand watching this meet in December 1933. In the background are the houses which are shown in the previous photograph.

By the 1930s plots of land around the Marton Hall estate were being sold off for building purposes. Here, we see some of the houses which were built at that time. Today this is The Grove, Marton.

Several fine halls and their estates existed in the local area. One shown here is the magnificent Marton Hall, c. 1910. Constructed for Henry Bolckow as a private residence in 1853, Bolckow moved here in 1856. He continued to improve the grandeur of the hall and its grounds where he planted many rare trees. He also amassed a fine art collection, later sold in London on 5 May 1888. The elegance of the hall was exemplified by its marble staircase and many other decorative features. When the twentieth century brought financial pressures for owners of these fine buildings, many were forced to sell them. The Middlesbrough area in particular has several examples. By the 1920s the hall was vacant and together with its grounds was purchased by Councillor T.D. Stewart and donated to the town for use as a park. Named after its donor, Stewart's Park is still very popular today although Marton Hall itself was demolished in 1960.

Another fine building which has disappeared is Tollesby Hall. Situated close to Marton, Tollesby Hall is thought to have been built in the early 1800s. Here in May 1930 its contents were being 'sold on the instructions of the late Mr E.B. Emmerson' whose father had bought it in 1886. In 1937, when Tollesby Hall was advertised as being for let at £200 per year, it was described as 'being in good repair … (with) four reception rooms, ten bedrooms, bathrooms, kitchens, garage and water and electric light both available.' After later becoming a builders yard, Tollesby Hall was eventually demolished in 1984.

Gunnergate Hall, a magnificent brick house built in Gothic style described by contemporary reports as a 'salubrious residence with a fine prospect' was built in 1857 for the Quaker banker, Charles Leatham. When he died within a year the house was purchased by John Vaughan, who with Henry Bolckow (then living in neighbouring Marton Hall) had been one of the leading figures in the development of Middlesbrough's iron industry. Vaughan himself died in 1868 after which the original house was greatly increased in size by his son Thomas. The house changed hands again in 1881 when Henry Bolckow's nephew, Carl, bought it following a rapid decline in the Vaughan fortunes after the crash of the iron industry two years earlier. Sir Raylton Dixon purchased the Hall in 1888 but when he died in 1901 the Hall remained unlived in apart from use by the army in both wars. Gunnergate Hall was eventually demolished in 1946.

When the Middlesbrough to Guisborough railway was constructed in 1854 its route passed between the Pennyman estate at Ormesby and the estate owned by Henry Bolckow at Marton Hall. A station was constructed where the railway bridged the country lane from Ormesby to Yarm. Shown here around 1906, Marton Station was then a much more substantial affair than its modern counterpart. The lane to Ormesby goes under the bridge while to the right is the lane that went around the eastern perimeter of the Marton estate.

For residents who remember Ormesby village in the days from before the Second World War, the memory is very much one of the classic country idyll. Certainly when this photograph was taken around 1910 it was a community unchanged for many years, essentially dependent upon an agricultural economy, a village of a few houses close to the Pennyman family home at Ormesby Hall. This scene includes the Red Lion public house on the left and Church Lane, the road to Guisborough, on the right.

Once again the quiet rural community of Ormesby is featured long before it became a part of the urban development of Middlesbrough. This view, from the other end of the village to that of the previous photograph, also looks towards the Red Lion public house. Today the ivy cottages close to the Red Lion have all been replaced by modern buildings.

126

One of the most memorable days in the history of Ormesby was on 17 July 1937 when the Prime Minister, the Rt Honourable Neville Chamberlain came to the village. He was to make an address to the Cleveland Unionists at a fete, presided over by the Marquis of Zetland, at Ormesby Hall. Apart from the attraction of seeing the Prime Minister there were many other activities for the crowds who attended.

Neville Chamberlain had only been Prime Minister since 28 May 1937. As expected, a large crowd gathered to see the new Prime Minister, most sitting in chairs on the lawn in front of the main house as they listened to his speech. Chamberlain, in his oratory, chose to ignore recent criticism of his policy of appeasement and instead attacked socialism. Incidentally the speech was relayed around the grounds by Uptons, a local company still in existence today.

GREAT TEES-SIDE DEMONSTRATION & FETE

AT

ORMESBY HALL

Near MIDDLESBROUGH

(Ormesby Station, L.N.E.R., five minutes)

SATURDAY, 17th JULY, 1937.

At 5.15 p.m. AN ADDRESS will be given by the

PRIME MINISTER

(The Rt. Hon. Neville Chamberlain, M.P.)

THE MARQUESS OF ZETLAND will preside

Reserved Seats for Mass Meeting 5/-, 2/6, & 1/- to be obtained from the Honorary Secretary.

REDCAR WORKS SILVER PRIZE BAND.

Amusements, Sideshows, Stalls

Dancing on Lawns, Hall Gardens Open to Public, Huge Marquee in case of showers.

AMPLE PARKING ACCOMMODATION

(A.A. Control)

Charas 2/6, Cars 1/-, Motor Cycles 3d. Ordinary Cycles Free.

TEA AND REFRESHMENTS in Large Marquees

GATES OPEN 2 p.m. to 8 p.m.

Admission Tickets 3d, if purchased before the day (6d at gate).

Tickets obtainable from any Tees-side Conservative Agent or Local Secretary.

Frequent Trains between Middlesbrough and Ormesby.

C. T. E. MASKELL, Hon. Sec.

16, WEST-TERRACE, REDCAR.

Make This Your Annual Outing.

Elaborate preparations had been taken to ensure that the event would have continued in the case of wet weather; a huge marquee, seating over 3,000 people, was erected close to the main house. However, a fine afternoon meant this wasn't needed and Chamberlain spoke from a platform out in the open air. He can be seen here on his way to the platform to make his speech, accompanied by Major J.B. Pennyman. During his visit to Ormesby Hall the post office made available a direct telephone line to Downing Street to keep Chamberlain in contact with Whitehall.

Chamberlain, shown here in the midst of his speech, received warm applause at the end. Afterwards he walked around the fete and although he was disappointed at not seeing Lingdale Sword Dancers, he was reported to be very impressed by the North Ormesby Morris dancers when they performed for him. It was quite a day for Ormesby. Very few people in Ormesby Hall on that afternoon could have any idea that a year later their guest would be on the front of newspapers across the world during the euphoria that followed the resolution of the Munich Crisis when Chamberlain was hailed as a national hero.